MIND
COSMOLOGY

MIND COSMOLOGY

Anthony Norvell

PARKER PUBLISHING COMPANY, INC.
West Nyack, N.Y.

Library of Congress
Catalog Card Number: 70-153946

PRINTED IN THE UNITED STATES OF AMERICA
ISBN -0-13-583260-8
B&P

DEDICATION

I dedicate this book to my lecture members and class students all over the world, who have been a source of inspiration and encouragement to me throughout the years.

Introduction

For centuries past, mystics, seers, holy men and prophets have taught a secret doctrine of tremendous mental and psychic powers that man may tap when he wishes to achieve astounding miracles in his life.

Now this secret doctrine, that comes to us from the Far East, has been proved to be accurate. In our modern scientific laboratories we are studying psychic phenomena, brain waves, and their healing effects upon the bodies of countless thousands; astral projection and the soul's living reality; the projection of mental and spiritual forces that are truly revolutionary in their effects on human destiny.

This book reveals for the first time, how you may use these wonderful cosmic laws, which are named Mind Cosmology, to perform everyday miracles such as attracting riches and abundance, and fulfilling your desired destiny in every aspect of your life.

By using this modern science of Mind Cosmology that combines the latest revelations of our space age with the age-old mystic truths of the Far East, you may program into your higher mind centers new and powerful creative ideas that will change your life as you want to live it immediately.

Do you desire a healthy, strong, youthful body, with unlimited vigor and energy? Mind Cosmology can show you how to tap the invisible wave lengths of life-giving cosmic energy that come to us from the billions of planets in outer space, and raise your rate of mental and physical vibrations so you are protected against germs and most forms of sickness.

3

Mind Cosmology sheds its rays of creative light in the minds of all those who know how to tune in on these cosmo-astral forces. Brilliant new patterns of thoughts will be yours; you will have psychic guidance, clairvoyant visions, and astral projection, when you learn how to channel these awesome cosmic forces into your own higher mind centers.

You Can Become a True Miracle Worker for Yourself

We are living in a miracle age, in which man has risen higher in this past hundred years than formerly in five thousand years. This is because man is at long last tapping these higher cosmic forces that existed for centuries in the invisible cosmos. You can become a true miracle worker, using these same laws and principles of Mind Cosmology.

If you apply Mind Cosmology with supreme faith that it can solve your problems, it can infuse you with a miracle-working power that can literally achieve for you anything that you desire.

You will be enabled to sharpen your sense-perceptions, so you will receive greater power for creative work. You may desire additional mental gifts for creating new objects, doing different work, or going into your own business; this can all be programmed into your mind centers by using the cosmic mind thermostat that you may set to any degree of success you wish.

You can set this psychic programmer on the achievement of a large sum of money, any amount you can believe in, from ten thousand to a million dollars and then let the cosmic programming be fulfilled in the most astonishing ways!

Through this one secret of Mind Cosmology you may achieve a fortune that can cause you to have financial security on any level of living you choose.

You can use this method of cosmic programming to secure a new car, a beautiful home, a complete wardrobe, jewels, furs, stocks and bonds, valuable lands, apartment houses, and success in your own business.

Is this too much to expect? Look about you at the world of

riches and abundance that this cosmic mind has created for you to use and enjoy. Realize that the world teems with riches and abundance. You can attract from the vast cornucopia of cosmic riches all the wealth you need to give you comfort, luxury, cultural benefits, world travel and other priceless treasures.

The Amazing Powers This Book Can Bestow Upon You

Mind Cosmology is the new science of the space age. It deals with the miraculous forces that exist in the invisible cosmos, which man may tap with his mind and channel to his everyday life for every constructive purpose.

This science is as old as time and space and yet as new as tomorrow's latest scientific revelations. It is a mystic power, combining in its revelations the oldest truths known to the mystics and seers of old, and the new, scientific discoveries of the atomic age.

Through Mind Cosmology you may cross the invisible, mystic threshold of consciousness and enter into another dimension of mind power. Through this mystical extension of the human mind and spirit you can channel the miracle-working power of a cosmic mind that operates in all nature.

In this atomic age man has blasted away the age-old superstitions and limitations of matter. He has released a miraculous, invisible power that is the most awesome of all his great discoveries.

Through the mystic power released by Mind Cosmology forces you may cross the mystic threshold of mind and spirit into the invisible cosmic realities of creative power.

The cosmic mind that created this universe and the billions of stars in the heavens, is a power that is available to you. You may tap this power and use it to achieve a great destiny for yourself.

What Mind Cosmology Can Do for You

1. You can tune your mind in on the wave lengths of the miraculous cosmic mind power that flows throughout the

cosmos. This mind power can give you creative intelligence to achieve anything that you desire.

2. You can use mind cosmology forces to program any destiny that you want through your higher creative mind centers, bringing you amazing success, happiness, peace of mind, love fulfillment and riches such as you never dreamed of attaining.

3. You will be shown how to use mind cosmology to tap a stratum of creative mind power that can bring you the greatest treasures of life. These include mental riches, material abundance, and the spiritual treasures of peace of mind and tranquility.

4. With the laws of mind cosmology you will learn how to solve all human problems and achieve cycles of good luck and prosperity even when others seem to have bad luck.

5. You will learn how to use the mind cosmology thermostat, to set any degree of success, happiness, and prosperity that you select.

6. You can use mind cosmology laws to program your body's good health, youthful energy and vitality for a hundred years or more of zestful living.

7. You can use this mystical power to send your soul into the cosmos through amazing astral projection, where you actually are able to travel backwards into the dim pages of history, or forward into the uncharted areas of future life experiences.

8. Your higher mind will be able to attune itself to the inspiring thought forms of the immortal masters who have lived before and who can give you ideas for inventions, songs, stories, art and business that can make you rich beyond your wildest dreams.

9. This study of the laws of mind cosmology will open mystical doors of the invisible and help you achieve an expanded cosmic consciousness in which the secrets of the ages will be known to you.

10. You will be shown in this study, how to use the mysterious power of psycho-kinesis to motivate matter and shape your destiny in any image that you choose. You can motivate people

to do your bidding; affect material substance and alter it, through this one dynamic secret alone.

11. Mind cosmology will reveal how you may use subconscious mind motivators to break the mold of past failures and misfortunes, and program a new set of positive experiences for your future.

12. You will be shown how to achieve cosmic perception, the ability to have psychic and clairvoyant vision; to read the thoughts of others, and to tap the cosmic mind that can give you psychic guidance and intuition to lead you to a glorious future.

13. You will be given secrets from the doctrines of the mystics of the Far East, that show you how to translate your inner dreams into the outer reality that you desire.

14. Mind cosmology will show you the method for achieving instant demonstrations of the things you want in life. Do you want a better job? More Money? A new home? A happier life? This secret doctrine can reveal all these glorious truths to you.

15. You will learn in this study of mind cosmology, of the cosmic stream of time and how you can motivate it to suit your needs. You can speed up time and make events happen in the eternal now, or you can slow down time and live a richer, fuller life, that will give you added years of enjoyment.

16. Mind cosmology can show you how to tap the cosmo-astral rays of the universe and put yourself in tune with healing forces that give you miracle-working powers. This knowledge can help keep your body healthy and strong; it uses the secrets of the ancients from India, China and Tibet, who knew how to control the body's life functions.

17. You will be shown how mind cosmology can magnetize and attract into your orbit of influence your true mate for love and marriage, and overcome the problems that often occur in marriage.

18. You will be guided for your mystic journey into the future dimensions of time and space, to reveal the destiny that is meant for you alone.

The Author

Contents

How to Tune in on the Miraculous Cosmic Mind Power That Meets All Your Needs

From the moment you were conceived as a thinking, breathing, living human being, some mystical cosmic power was at work shaping your invisible blueprint of destiny to meet all your needs.

This invisible intelligence flows throughout the cosmic spaces, creating all things, and motivating all life. In this study of Mind Cosmology, you will be shown how to tap this amazing cosmic mind and channel it to your every need in life.

For centuries the mystics of the Far East have known that a cosmic force exists which shapes all creation. They teach that there is a cosmic spirit in the universe which is back of all generative action. Just as man possesses a soul which permeates his body, so too the cosmos possesses a soul or spirit, which permeates all things in the universe. When this cosmic spirit or mind is contacted by man, then the cells of his brain and body become infused with a creative life force that is capable of creating anything man desires.

How This Cosmic Mind Creates in Nature

We see this creative cosmic mind working in the realm of nature shaping all visible and invisible forces.

When it wants to create a flower it draws upon the cosmic mind memory bank, where there are millions of varieties of flowers stored as electronic and atomic impulses. A rose is different from an orchid or a daffodil; the cosmic mind knows how to create each species according to this invisible cosmic mind pattern.

When you want to create something in your own life, you can draw upon this cosmic mind power and cause it to release the secret force within your mind and body which will show you how to create it.

This cosmic mind power works in nature through four levels of consciousness:

1. The human
2. The vegetable
3. The animal
4. The mineral.

The mineral kingdom has atomic action within its structure, but it has no mind power, cannot move about of its own free will, and lacks reproductive powers. Its creative action is limited.

Some people operate on this level of consciousness; they have little will power; they let life push them around; they stay on one job, which they may hate, for years, lacking the initiative to make a change. They remain in fixed incomes that may not be adequate, and they have little vision for the future.

Then other people operate on the level of the vegetable kingdom. The vegetable has growth, living cells, can reproduce its kind, but is stationary and cannot choose the destiny it desires.

Haven't you seen people who operate on this limited level of existence? They vegetate mentally; they never have a new idea, they never try to rise above their limitations; they accept whatever comes their way but never initiate any new mental action that could profoundly change their lives for the better.

How One Woman Used Mind Cosmology to Change Her Life

Sarah H. was a woman in her fifties, when she first came into our study of mind cosmology and metaphysics. She had lost her husband through death, her children were grown up and on their own, and she was just vegetating in life. She had let herself get heavy and had become careless in her dress habits. She had no interest in anything or anyone, and told me in our first interview that she did not know what she was living for.

My first impression of Sarah H. was of a very old and very tired woman without purpose or direction in life. She told me that she would never marry again, and she had no outstanding interests in life.

I immediately put Sarah H. on a Mind Cosmology program, which she was to follow religiously for two weeks. She was to change her entire philosophy of life; instead of seeing herself as being finished in life she was to visualize herself just beginning a new life.

She was to release cosmic mind motivators into her higher consciousness, which would activate the creative centers of her brain. These were:

1. A desire to attract a mate and have another happy marriage.
2. A desire to give something of value to the world.
3. A desire to help other people who were less fortunate than herself.
4. A desire to make money in some activity where she could give of her services and receive something in return.

Sarah H. began to concentrate on these motivating forces

every day in an hour session of meditation. She began to act out in her imagination the fulfillment of the new dream that I had implanted in her consciousness.

Within two weeks time Sarah H. had changed in an amazing way. She was aflame with a new and intense desire to live and have a great future and a new life.

She began to be more active socially, and soon was meeting people who were doing things that were constructive and creative. She went to a big social event and there met a retired doctor who was soon courting her; the first step in her new mind cosmology blueprint. She then began to channel the second desire, the desire to give something of value to the world. Soon she was working with a hospital that her doctor friend had formerly been associated with, helping in the out-patient department as a social worker, giving freely of her time and effort. Soon Sarah H. was so occupied that her life became full and joyous. When the doctor proposed marriage she was happy to accept him, and they were married.

With her help and inspiration the retired doctor returned to his former practice and was more successful than ever before; thus bringing into focus the other two facets of Sarah H's cosmic mind motivators; a desire to help other people, and a desire to make money in some activity where she could give of her services and receive something in return.

Now in her beautiful new home, Sarah H. was hostess to the many friends they both had, and in her husband's offices, she was the receptionist, assisting him in his work, and helping sick people find health and happiness. This gave her such joy that her entire life took on new meaning and purpose.

Take These Three Steps to Change Your Life Through Mind Cosmology

1. Be aware that you were created for a great destiny and that you can fulfill it with the help of your higher mind.
2. Start today to think, talk, look and act important, so you will release to the world an image of value and greatness.

3. Search within each day to find your hidden potentials and creative gifts which you can release to the world.

When you once make up your mind that you will align yourself with the cosmic mind power that creates all things, you will instantly begin to think, act, talk and look more successful. You will feel the inflow of this creative mind power and it will help inspire you to great deeds.

Everywhere you look in nature you see this cosmic mind power expressing its creative force. See how beautifully a rose unfolds its petals to a newborn day, fully aware that it has a message of beauty and fragrance to give to the world.

See how magnificently a giant tree rears it branches to heaven, as though supplicating the sun and moon and stars for the heavenly vision to make it great.

See how beautifully a new baby reaches out its little arms to grasp its loving mother, intuitively knowing that it will find security, food and shelter there.

See how gloriously all nature is attuned to the rhythm of this cosmic mind power, in the ebb and flow of the tides; in the celestial carousel where billions of planets revolve in their orbits without collision or confusion.

See the rhythm which this cosmic mind expresses in nature; spring, with its planting of seed; summer, with its growth and fruition; fall with its harvest of the crops; and winter for the earth's restful pause from its creative cycles.

Cosmic Mind Has Made Joyous Provision for Your Future

This higher cosmic mind has made joyous provision for your sustenance in the future. Under the great cosmic law of gravity and magnetism, the life force flows earthward which gives you health and energy and long life. When you work with this law of magnetic attraction you can use Mind Cosmology laws to attract into your orbit, just as the stars do, whatever you vibrate to magnetically. You can put into your higher cosmic mind centers magnetic thoughts of money, and you will soon become rich.

You can project the magnetic desire for friends and your life will be blessed with people who think as you do. Like attracts like; this is a law of magnetic attraction.

You can project this cosmic mind power of magnetism to your body cells and fill them with life, health, youth and energy.

Truly, you can become a miracle worker when you once attune your higher mind centers to this cosmic mind which knows all, sees all, is all powerful and knows how to create everything you desire for the future.

How Anna L. Changed Her Life Through Laws of Mind Cosmology

A student of mine, Anna L. in New York City, worked for a law firm. She wanted to advance and become financially independent. She took the three steps above and started to work with cosmic mind power.

One day in meditation Anna L. had a sudden inspiration. The thought came through: Why don't you open a bureau of legal stenographers, who can write briefs for various law firms?

Anna L. started her legal stenographic service in which she had two other girls working with her. They did lawyer's briefs for beginning lawyers, who could not afford their own secretaries. Soon they had so many attorneys using their services that Anna L. had to engage three more secretaries and she was making more money than she had ever thought possible before.

You Are Bigger Than You Think!

You actually have hidden potentials and possibilities for the future that can bring you anything you desire in life. Mind Cosmology helps you focus this power in your higher mind centers.

A young man I knew was married and the father of three children, but he could never make much money as a mechanic. He needed a bigger income, so when he came into our study work, he learned how Mind Cosmology could help him achieve his goals in life. He was especially impressed by the second giant step: The ability to think, talk, look and act important.

I gave Joe K. a mental regime to follow. In his work as a mechanic he was to treat every customer as though he, Joe, owned the service station. He was to show concern for the customer's welfare, and to project an air of importance.

Soon Joe K. was selling more gas and giving better service than the other employees. In four weeks he was made manager of the service station, with a substantial raise in salary. In two months time a man came into the station with a big Cadillac. He was having carburetor trouble. Joe showed such genuine interest and did such a good job for the man that when it came time to pay his bill the man asked Joe for his telephone number. Two days later this wealthy man called Joe at his home and told him he was opening a big service station and wanted Joe to be a partner. He said, "I was impressed by your attitude toward me, your honesty and ability, and I need someone like you to work with me."

Without any capital, Joe went to work with this man and soon he was a full-time partner in a most profitable business. Now Joe owns a beautiful home in the country; his children are assured of a fine education, he drives a beautiful car and his every dream is on the way to coming true.

Cosmic Mind Power Flows According to Your Needs

It is a truism in mind cosmology that cosmic mind power flows to your own higher mind centers according to your needs.

If you want to make a million dollars, there is a cosmic mind formula somewhere in the cosmic memory bank that can make you a millionaire. In the past few years there have been over twenty thousand new millionaires created in the United States. Don't let anyone tell you that it is impossible to get rich now because of big taxes or any other reason.

The Mysterious "Other" Mind That Works for You

There is a mysterious "other" mind that works for you

twenty-four hours a day. It is the cosmic intelligence which releases the power to your conscious and subconcious mind centers. It tells your heart how to beat all night, without your being aware of it; it digests your food, without any effort on your part. It heals your body, repairs the tissues of the body, causes you to breathe automatically. It kills invading bacteria that might make you sick. This cosmic mind motivates your memory, your imagination, your sense perceptions. This "other" mind is truly a miracle worker and it can be used by you to do other, amazing things even outside your body.

Step-by-Step Guide for Using Cosmic Mind Power to Meet All Your Needs

1. Cosmic mind power cannot work through your higher mind centers and it cannot give you psychic vision and intuitive guidance if your mind is filled with negative thoughts.

Clear your mind first of all negative thoughts. Give yourself a positive treatment every morning when you start your day by saying to yourself such positive statements as the following:

> I am now in a positive state of mind. I eradicate all negative thoughts from my past. I do not accept failure and fear and worry as my natural lot in life. I am a spiritual being with a divine soul. I now expand my mind to receive cosmic mind power and I am successful. I am healthy. I am youthful and energetic. I am radiantly happy. I have a great destiny to look forward to.

2. Then when you have set your mental state for positive action, give yourself a mental blueprint of the things you wish cosmic mind power to do for you.

Write down on a piece of paper what you want to demonstrate for yourself through the use of cosmic mind power.

> Do you want to use it to improve your gifts?
> Do you want to use this power to make a fortune?
> Do you desire love happiness, a marriage, a home of your own?
> Do you want this power to go into your own business?

3. When you have decided exactly what you want the cosmic mind to do for you, make out your personal blueprint of destiny, similar to the following:

MY COSMIC BLUEPRINT OF DESTINY

I ask cosmic mind to show me how to achieve the following things. I have faith that this power can bring me anything that I desire.

I wish to be a personal success; to have a strong, magnetic personality that wins and holds friends.

I wish to become financially successful. I want to attract $10,000 for more security and comfort. I wish the bigger sum of $100,000 for an over-all goal of security for the future. I wish to demonstrate this sum in the next ten years.

A lady in my Los Angeles lecture group set up a similar blueprint asking that she sell a piece of property that no one seemed to want to buy. Within two weeks time someone bought the property, paying her exactly what she was asking! When you crystallize your ideas of money and success in definite patterns of thought, the cosmic mind that knows all secrets, somehow guides you to fulfill the destiny you choose.

Another student of mine, using these laws of cosmic mind power asked for $100,000 within three months time. But he did not have faith that this could come to him so quickly, and it did not. He told me of his disappointment, and I told him to change his blueprint to read at first, that he wanted the sum of $1,000. Within two months time, he had his $1,000, and then went on with new faith to his bigger goals, scaling them upwards as he had more faith in the cosmic mind power.

Then add other desires to that cosmic blueprint, such as:

I would like to own my own business. (Here you must select whether you want a restaurant, a beauty shop, a manufacturing center, a book store, or a dance hall. Cosmic mind can guide you better if you come to it with specific requests.)

I would like to ask cosmic mind to attract me to my true soul mate with the following qualities. (Here state the type of soul mate you desire, giving the mental traits and character you admire most in a mate.)

Georgia R. did this in her blueprint of destiny. She wrote, "I wish to meet a man, tall, blue-eyed, good education, either in law or medicine, with a loving nature and a steady income."

She visualized meeting this ideal mate every night. She mentally passed pictures through her mind of dancing with her dream man, marrying him, living in her dream home.

One night Georgia R. was invited to a party at a friend's home. Half an hour after she arrived something made her look up at the door to the living room; there stood a tall, handsome, blonde man with blue eyes. He walked directly to her, as though impelled by some higher power. They were introduced by the host, and instantly felt as though they had known each other for years. This young man sought out Georgia R. during the next few weeks, and they went to many social events. He proposed marriage to her and they had a June wedding. The young man turned out to be a junior partner in a law firm, and made a very good salary.

4. Cosmic mind power exists all around you; it is in the air you breathe, it is in your own higher mind centers; you need only concentrate on it and it will reveal itself to you.

To attune your higher mind centers to this cosmic mind, make out a daily schedule in which you select the events, persons and situations you wish to occur for that day. This is a miniature blueprint for your daily affairs. You can list the sales you want to make, if you are a salesman. You can put down the names of people you want to meet socially. You can write down smaller sums of money you wish from unexpected sources; trips you want to take; creative ideas you wish to express; talents you want to have; and songs, stories, inventions, or other creative thoughts that you would like to receive from this higher cosmic mind.

An artist friend of mind sits every day, early in the morning, scheduling his actions for that day. He runs through his mind the mental images of the scenes he wants cosmic mind to paint through him. Soon his hands feel an irresistible urge to grasp the brushes and he paints as though under control of a master.

An author I know never writes a word until he has gone

through this cosmic mind programming. He has studied with me, and knows that some higher mind can write through him. When the flow of words starts he never stops until it ends. He has written three successful novels, all made into successful films.

5. To tune in on cosmic mind power that can meet all your needs, you must remove the negative barriers from your subconscious and conscious minds that impede the flow of your higher psychic mind centers. Each night go over your life from the earliest days you can remember. Each time you come across an unpleasant or negative emotional barrier, reason out this experience and remove it by substituting a pleasant memory for it.

Run through your mind all the shocks, tragedies, illnesses, accidents, failures, losses of money or loved ones—everything that has been stored in your subconscious as a negative force, and remove it by giving yourself positive suggestions to take the place of these negative ones.

Some of these positive subconscious suggestions you may use are:

> I remove all negative mental ghosts from my mind. I now substitute in their place positive mental forces. I realize the past is gone and cannot affect me. I now operate in the eternal now and fill my mind with only positive thoughts. I remove the mental blocks of failure and substitute success. I remove all past experiences of accident, sickness, misery, and failure and in their place I substitute security, health, happiness and success. I remove all hate, fear and worry and in their place I imprint thoughts of faith, confidence, joy and radiance.

A young woman I know had a very bitter and unhappy childhood. It kept her from being normal and expressing love and happiness fully. She was thirty and had never married because her mother had told her how brutal all men were. When this woman learned how Mind Cosmology could give her a new life she got rid of her mental and emotional ghosts and began to live in a new awareness of life. She soon attracted love and marriage and now has two fine sons and is extremely happy.

SUMMARY OF CHAPTER ONE

1. How to shape your blueprint of destiny for cosmic mind power to manifest for you a bright future.

2. The four invisible kingdoms through which cosmic mind power is expressed and how to raise yourself to the highest.

3. The amazing powers possessed by your higher mind when you tap the cosmic mind that knows all, sees all and is all.

4. How great creative minds have channeled this cosmic mind power to perform their wondrous feats in art, music, literature, invention and discovery.

5. The three giant steps you can take that will release more of this cosmic mind power in your creative mind centers.

6. How one woman used mind cosmology to create her own business and triple her income as a legal secretary.

7. How one man who was a mechanic attracted a backer in his own business and became successful and rich.

8. How you may tap the mysterious "other" mind that can show you how to become anything you desire.

9. How to create your own cosmic blueprint of destiny that can bring you your heart's desires.

10. How one young man attracted the sum of money he asked for in a very short time by using cosmic mind power.

11. How one woman asked cosmic mind for her true soul mate, met him and married him, achieving her life dream.

12. How to attune your mind to this higher cosmic mind and choose the events, persons and conditions you want in your future life.

2

How to Program the Destiny
You Want Through
Mind Cosmology

Through the science of Mind Cosmology you can program an entire new set of experiences into your higher mind centers, creating any destiny that you desire.

Are you dissatisfied with your lot in life?

Do you long for a better job?

Are you anxious to make more money and have financial security?

Are you bored with your daily living routine?

Do you long for fulfillment in love and marriage?

Do you want a wide circle of friends and a better social life?

Are you anxious to develop creative talents, such as painting, writing, inventing, composing, where you can become famous and rich?

If you have a desire for any of these things you can achieve them. You can use Mind Cosmology to program into your higher mind centers anything you really desire, and the cosmic mind of the universe, working through natural laws, begins to bring these desires into focus.

Activated Desire Is the Secret Key
to Cosmic Programming

The secret key that opens mystical doors to the hidden treasures of the universe is activated desire. When you long for something with intense emotion, you release magnetic and electrical forces within your mind which direct you to the fulfillment of the goals you desire.

See how this principle works in nature. In the maple seed, for example, cosmic mind has programmed the atoms with invisible roots, branches, trunk, and even the little capillaries which are to carry the sap from roots to branches—they are all there, written in the atomic structure of that maple seed like a program photographed on microfilm. The maple seed has an intense desire to become a tree and when put into the ground, it achieves that destiny.

The Miracle You Are Was Cosmically Programmed

You too possess this cosmic key within the cells of your brain and body. The miracle that you are was cosmically programmed into your father's and mother's genes and cells by some higher cosmic intelligence. The color of your hair and eyes, the height you were to become, the characteristics you were to have, and all other data was programmed within those genes of the destiny you would come into, the talents you were to develop. They are all there, your hidden potentials, waiting to spring into fruition the moment you call upon your higher mind centers.

If you have negatively programmed yourself since birth, you can break the mold of past negative habits and change that cosmic programming so you can become anything you wish to be.

Some people are programmed negatively by their parents, by education, by newspapers and television, so they become altered in their original pure patterns of creative thought. When this happens they develop into inferior, weak and unhappy individuals.

Negative Programming Caused This Man to Become an Alcoholic

Lester M. came into my work in New York City in a shocking mental and physical condition from constant drinking. He wanted help so I gave him an interview and learned his tragic story.

When he was young his father drank excessively. He beat his wife, and finally ran off and left his family. The boy's psychic centers were programmed with those daily scenes of bickering, confusion and horror and his subconscious was set in that negative mold. When he was sixteen Lester began drinking, and by the time he was twenty he was a chronic alcoholic.

Lester married when he was twenty-two and he repeated the cycle that had been programmed into his subconscious mind by his father. There were scenes of fighting and violence, and when they had a child, his wife finally left, taking their year-old son.

I gave Lester the mind cosmology programming that I knew would help him break the habit patterns of the past. He repeated positive programming statements, which were simple statements of positive action, such as, "I now break the mold of past habit patterns. I am no longer under the drive to escape my problems through using alcohol. I now program new habit patterns into my subconscious mind. I am strong. I want to change my life. I will stop drinking. I will organize my life once again to express the cosmic plan of perfection, happiness, health and fulfillment."

This cosmic programming worked wonders for Lester. He returned to me in four weeks time, clean-shaven, well-dressed, and told me he had joined Alcoholics Anonymous. He had found work, his wife and son returned to him and he swore that he would live a different life from that time on.

The Positive Way to Program Your New Destiny

1. If you have been programmed negatively in the past, you must begin to break the mold of past subconscious habits and build the new Mind Cosmology patterns of positive action. You can be helped to do this by using what we call cosmic circuit-breakers to reach into your mind centers and change your habit patterns.

Following Are the Mind Cosmology Circuit-Breakers

The circuit breaker of faith in a higher power.
The circuit-breaker of unselfish service.
The circuit-breaker of love.
The circuit-breaker of a desire for a better life.
The circuit-breaker of positive affirmations.
The circuit-breaker of dedication to a higher life.
The circuit-breaker of prayer and invocation.

2. To begin your positive mind cosmology regime to break past negative programming, begin on your first day to use the circuit-breaker of faith in a higher power.

Write down on a little card, which you carry with you, this affirmation: "I now have faith in the power of cosmic mind to overcome all my problems. I overcome fear, worry and hate, and all other negative forces that have been programmed into me. I affirm my oneness with God and His divine protection is now mine."

Then memorize the twenty-third Psalm and the ninety-first Psalm, and whenever you feel discouraged, worried or insecure, repeat these two powerful Psalms over and over until calm is restored.

3. Express your faith daily by looking about you at the evidences of how this cosmic mind works in nature, through the laws of the cosmos. Align yourself with that higher power by starting each day with the circuit-breaker of faith and prayer. When you open your eyes each morning, thank God for life. Dedicate your every living breath to God in the service of humanity.

A salesman of household articles, such as refrigerators, vacuum cleaners, stoves and utensils, approached every customer with such a positive attitude. He said a silent prayer that he could give something of value to his customers. As he expressed this silent prayer or wish, his brain centers were so charged with dynamic cosmic power that he sold nearly one hundred percent more articles than the other salesmen!

4. Daily, program into your higher psychic centers the circuit-breaker of unselfish service. Follow the cosmic law of giving. Give your talents, your creative energy, your time, your consideration, your encouragement, your smiles, your friendship, all with the thought that you are helping the world. You will, under the great cosmic law of reciprocity, receive in return something in equal value to what you have given out.

How a Sick Woman Was Healed with This Principle

Dora T. was nearly sixty, and very sick, when she sought out my help through Mind Cosmology. Her husband was dead, she had no children, and the doctors had told her she had an incurable ailment that would get progressively worse. This blow shattered her morale and she lost her reason for living.

In helping this woman I immediately used two circuit-breakers to help overcome the past negative programming of belief in age, sickness, loneliness and loss. I built her faith in God, and then gave her the circuit-breaker of unselfish service to use in her daily life. She immediately began to break the old mold of grief, worry, and fear of the future.

Dora T. had no financial problems, as she had been left well-off by her husband, but she had hours of time on her hands to worry and fret. I told her to go to Veteran's organizations and offer her services; to register with the Lighthouse for the Blind, and read for blind people, or do other work for them. I sent her to the New York Foundling's Home, where she worked four hours a week with children. Within four weeks time Dora T. returned to me a completely changed person. Her face was brighter in expression, her symptoms of sickness had decreased, and she was happier than she had been for years. As she became more concerned about the problems of others, she forgot her own burdens and actually became happier and healthier.

5. Use the circuit-breaker of love to help you. Love is a healing force. If you have been negatively programmed to a life of emotional frustration, you need to release more of this healing emotion in your daily life. Each day practice sending out loving thoughts to every one you meet. When someone presents an attitude of resentment, hate or envy, project at once the emotion of love. Think to yourself, "I now send you love and you will respond with love."

A school teacher used the circuit-breaker of love as follows:

Joyce D. was a teacher in first year high school. Her students were boisterous and refused to obey her. She tried to be stern and demand obedience, but things got worse and worse.

When Joyce D. came to me for help, I instantly told her what was wrong. She had been programmed with the ideas that firmness, discipline, and severity must be used to handle children.

I told Joyce, "See your students as human beings, with individual problems. Each one needs love. Perhaps in their homes they face problems that now reflect in their aggressive, belligerent personalities. Radiate love in your thoughts, your voice and expression, and soon you will see a change in your pupils."

Joyce D. reported back in two weeks that there was indeed a change in her students' mental attitude! Instead of becoming angry at her students Joyce began to smile more, and showed more sympathy and understanding. She poured out love to each student and they couldn't resist the emotion of love that now motivated their teacher. There was more harmony in the classroom than there had ever been before.

6. The circuit-breaker of desire can help you to a richer and better life. Most people believe that the forces of life are against them, not for them. They believe they must have bad luck, be

sick, be poor, unhappy, and that things must go wrong for them.

It is now known psychologically that a belief in bad luck, sickness and accident, actually programs the subconscious mind with negative forces that cause such unwanted conditions.

Desire success and you will program success into your higher centers of the subconscious mind.

Desire health and long life, and your cells will be imprinted with the life force that gives you health and longevity.

Desire money, fame, riches, and soon you will become programmed to attract these things into your life experience.

A college student used this method of cosmic programming to help him get better grades. He consistently got low grades in his first year of college. I gave him a program to use to change his mental attitude from failure to success. Each night when he went to sleep, he programmed into his subconscious mind the desire to excel in his studies and be first in his class. Within one month he began getting higher grades and in his second year he surpassed all other members of his class. He later graduated cum laude and became one of New York's brightest young attorneys.

7. Use the circuit-breaker of positive affirmations.

To help break past negative programming, use positive affirmations every time you feel you need them. Memorize these circuit-breakers and repeat them often each day.

> I affirm that I am now in the orbit of power and energy. I am surrounded by a magnetic field of positive life force. I am vital and strong. My mind is now programmed with success. I project an attitude of loving co-operation and attract friends. I overcome all discouragement and defeat. I have faith in myself and my ability to succeed. I affirm that I am healthy and resistant to all disease. I believe I will make a fortune. I live in an aura of dynamic magnetism and positive power. I attract health, happiness, love, friendship, and prosperity.

A Great California Artist Uses This Method to Paint

An inferior artist a few years ago came into my study classes in California and began to use a positive programming affirmation I gave him before he began each canvas. He would sit quietly and affirm to himself:

> I now draw upon the creative mind of the Master Artist of the Cosmos, God. He created all things and knows how to paint a perfect picture through me. His masterpiece is in the cerulean blue of the skies, the ultramarine of the seas, the pink and white of a delicate rose. He has created the greens of trees, shrubs and plants. His palette is aflame with the incandescent gold and crimson of a flaming sunset; His beauty is stamped upon the entire universe and I shall capture this image of loveliness in my work today.

This man is now considered one of the finest landscape artists in Southern California.

8. Use the circuit-breaker of dedication to a higher life.

The science of Mind Cosmology teaches that you were born to a higher destiny than ordinary mortals. You have divine potentials within your soul. You must believe this. You must dedicate your mind and body as channels to serve God and humanity and great creative power will flow through your mind.

How a Salesman Used Cosmic Dedication to Make a Fortune

A salesman who had been a failure, came into a study of Mind Cosmology in our study group in New York. He had an inferior concept of his ability as a salesman. He sold life insurance and felt guilty about telling people they needed his product. After he had been trained in Mind Cosmology, he began to change his entire attitude. He broke the negative programming with the circuit-breaker of dedication. He told himself that he was selling a valuable product that gave families protection and security for the future. He gave himself a positive treatment each day when he set out to work. "I dedicate myself to giving something of value to the world. I realize my product is valuable and offers protection to families in time of need. I give something of value and in return I receive value. I joyously dedicate myself to doing good for humanity. This day

I set forth to conquer life and achieve good for myself and others."

Another young man who was in advertising work changed his entire life by using this type of psychic programming. He dedicated himself to serving his clients, and soon received three raises. Every night when he goes to bed, he gives his subconscious mind programming that he will succeed, that he will help his family and the world, and he asks for cosmic mind to guide him in his every move the following day.

9. Use the circuit-breaker of prayer and invocation to help you program a great destiny.

Faith and prayer are a powerful combination for programming your higher mind centers for greatness.

When you feel discouraged or suffer from the negative effects of past programming, which causes you defeat, failure, sickness or discouragement, try retiring for a few moments into the innermost cathedral of your soul, and say a short prayer. You may use the well-known prayer, "Our Father, which art in heaven . . . " or say the twenty-third psalm, or make up a short prayer of your own.

A stockbroker who had studied Mind Cosmology in my classes in New York told me that he never goes a day without saying short prayers for guidance in his difficult work. His mind centers seem to be clear and accurate, and his psychic powers have made many of his clients rich.

When you keep your mind in attunement with the cosmic mind that rules the invisible and visible universe, you receive divine guidance through your psychic centers as to the right course of action to follow in your daily life.

SUMMARY OF CHAPTER TWO

1. How to program an entirely new life through the laws of mind cosmology and bring new experiences into focus.

2. How to use the key of activated desire to achieve complete psychic and cosmic programming of your destiny.

3. How negative programming produces sickness, accident,

failure and unhappiness, and what to do to change it to positive programming.

4. How one man became an alcoholic through the negative programming he received when he was a child.

5. The seven circuit-breakers to shatter the past mold of negative programming and rebuild a complete new cycle of positive experiences.

6. How Dora T. used Mind Cosmology to shatter the mold of sickness, despair and defeat and built a new life of health, happiness and fulfillment.

7. How you can use the circuit-breaker of love to bring you into dynamic new dimensions of human experience.

8. The circuit-breaker of desire for a better life and how it brought a businessman success and fortune.

9. How to use the circuit-breakers of positive affirmations to program health, money, love and happiness.

10. An artist, using the circuit-breaker of desire, became famous and rich by creating magnificent paintings.

11. How one man used the circuit-breaker of dedication to get bigger ideas for his business. He had three raises in salary in a short time.

12. How the circuit-breaker of prayer and invocation works to put you into attunement with the cosmic mind that created all things and knows how to guide you through your psychic centers.

How to Use Cosmic Protoplasm
to Create Unlimited
Riches and Abundance

The cosmic spaces of the entire universe are filled with an invisible spiritual protoplasm that creates everything we see in the visible and invisible universe.

Knowledge of this great cosmic secret can help you draw upon the cosmic storehouse of riches and abundance. You have the power to use Mind Cosmology to materialize treasures of the mind, body, soul, and to enrich your life beyond your present comprehension, by having all the money you need to furnish you with every comfort and luxury you demand of life.

This chapter tells you how you can use this cosmic protoplasm to create unlimited riches and abundance in every department of your life.

How This Cosmic Abundance Flows in All Nature

See how mysteriously and miraculously this cosmic abundance flows to all creatures in the realm of nature.

Deep in the sea cosmic mind has created algae to feed many species of fish; strange plants grow there that furnish the life-giving oxygen and food for thousands of varieties of creatures of the deep.

In the earth above the seas cosmic mind has planted a variety of shrubs, trees, bushes and herbs to furnish mankind with lumber to build his homes; nourishing food to keep his body alive and functioning in perfect health; medicines to heal him if he should be sick; materials to weave clothing to keep him warm; elements and minerals in the soil, such as coal, gold, oil, silver, platinum, and atomic energy. In the seas and in the soil this cosmic protoplasm has formed diamonds, pearls, emeralds, rubies, sapphires and other precious stones to adorn mankind and furnish him with beauty and pleasure.

Can such an intelligence, that has so amply provided for man's needs ever be thought of as poor, limited or lacking? Mankind can, when it has learned how to harness this tremendous cosmic force, produce everything it will ever need to sustain itself on this earth for many generations to come.

How You May Use Cosmic Power Motivators
to Bring Riches to You

The invisible cosmic protoplasm that fills the entire universe may be motivated and shaped by the power of your mind. Through Mind Cosmology you may form mental thought forms and project them into this invisible cosmic protoplasm and cause it to materialize in your life in any shape that you desire.

What are these cosmic power motivators that can bring you riches? There are many and you may choose those you wish for your own particular demonstration of what you desire in your life.

Cosmic Power Motivator Number One
The Unselfish Desire to Help Your Family
Achieve a Better Life

When you use this cosmic motivator to spur you on to the

achievement of success you are using one of the most basic of all forces in Mind Cosmology.

Man does not live for himself alone; he lives for others as well as for himself. To tap the cornucopia of vast cosmic treasures you must have some creative idea to inspire you to achieve your goal. To want to help your family, to educate your children, to give them a better way of life, is one of life's most inspiring forces.

When you project this idea to cosmic mind, it begins to shape the invisible spiritual and cosmic protoplasm in the direction of your goal-striving.

Project this idea onto paper; write down what you want for your family; the house you want to own; the land you wish to have; the car you want for their enjoyment and comfort; the security you wish, putting down the sums of money you want in the bank to give them everything they need; the health, happiness, prosperity that you feel they deserve.

When you crystallize your cosmic mind force with *definiteness* and project these ideas constantly, they magnetize the elements you need for your life-fulfillment.

Cosmic Power Motivator Number Two

The Ego-Drive to Achieve Your Life Goal

Within every one of God's creatures there is an innate desire to express itself as a living, loving, creating being. This urge that the cosmic spirit has implanted within you is known in psychology as the ego-drive. Mind Cosmology recognizes this dominant principle in the human psyche and strives to release the ego-urge in a positive, constructive way.

Most people have the ego-urge in a selfish, self-centered way and are often boastful, arrogant and dominating, feeling they have a right to make demands on life and people. This is the wrong type of ego expression and violates the basic cosmic law of identity and self-recognition.

When this ego-drive to achieve your life goal is properly motivated, you will strive to express only the best of your personality.

You will put into your mind superior thoughts and they will build true superiority without arrogance.

You will release in your personality qualities of kindness, unselfishness, charity and good, and your magnetism will increase, attracting to you persons who are of the same mental caliber.

You will take pride in yourself and your work, and improve the quality of your mind and personality, so they will reflect value in whatever work you do. In this way you will quickly win recognition and rise rapidly to a high position in life.

How One Young Woman Became Inspired to Achieve Greatness

A young woman who had studied these mental laws of Cosmology, decided she would use her talents to help poor, unfortunate people. She wanted to do something for others, but as she did not have much money, being an office worker, she did not know how to go about it. In a period of meditation one day, in which she asked her higher, cosmic mind to help her, she was told to become a social worker. She went out to her community center that same day and applied for work and was immediately accepted. Now this young lady is doing work that is interesting and will lead her to the goal-achievement she desired.

How an Actor Used the Cosmic Urge of Ego-Drive for Success

A young actor in Hollywood, to whom I had given these cosmic principles was very conceited and arrogant at first. He lost many movie roles because of this trait, and later when he learned the art of releasing the true ego-drive of unselfish good, he changed his entire attitude and became one of Hollywood's biggest stars. The press, that had formerly hated him and called him conceited, now changed and helped make him one of the best-loved stars in the world.

The Five Simple Steps for Achieving Ego-Drive

1. Never think of yourself as being superior unless you *really* are.
2. Build your inner and outer qualities until they reflect true value to the outer world.
3. Practice restraint in making demands on others, bossing people, dominating your friends, and gain their willing co-operation by asking them for favors and winning their approval and support.
4. Stand before your mirror each day before beginning your day's work and affirm, "I am surrounded by the Magic Circle of God's Divine Love. I reflect only His qualities of goodness, beauty, peace and divine love in my personality. I magnetize and attract into my orbit of experience only those persons who vibrate to the same qualities of the divine mind."
5. Dedicate yourself every day when you start your day to being a channel for God to work through. Adopt the divine will for your will and let this cosmic power express itself in your personality as self-confidence, without arrogance; as strength, without boastfulness or dominance.

How an Insurance Salesman Increased His Sales
100% with Ego-Drive

An insurance salesman came into our work and learned of the principles of Mind Cosmology, especially the five simple steps for achieving ego-drive. He had been one of the worst salesmen in his company and had seriously thought of giving up his work. He had tried to have an overpowering personality, with plenty of egotism and dominance, but people shied clear of him. Then he realized what had been wrong; he had been forcing his ego on others, and not really using ego-drive as it should be. He changed his tactics, he began to really become interested in his clients and their welfare; he stopped forcing himself on people, but let them make advances to him. He started each day's work with an affirmation made before his mirror which stated,

"Today I shall be the best salesman in the world. I shall constantly keep my clients' interests and welfare in the forefront of my mind. I shall sell every prospect I meet today."

This formula worked wonders for this man. In just one month's time his sales jumped twenty-five percent; in six months he was selling more insurance than anyone in his company, and he now stands to make fifty thousand dollars a year from the policies he sells!

Cosmic Power Motivator Number Three

Choose a Life Work That You Take Pride in Doing

There is nothing more inspiring than being in work that you sincerely enjoy. If your work is drudgery, you cannot draw on the cosmic magnetism and power to make you a success. It is better to get out of it and supply yourself with the cosmic power motivator that gives you pride in your work.

I knew a forty-year-old man who was in factory work, operating a punch press, which he detested. He kept at his job for many years because he had three growing children and a wife to support. When he learned the principles of cosmology and the importance of using this cosmic power motivator of taking pride in his work, he decided he would change his work, regardless of how many years he had been in it. He asked his higher psychic mind for guidance; he had always wanted to be in work that had to do with animals, for he had always loved dogs and had two family pets that his family adored. He was guided to a man one day who was in the dog-training business, and who had a home in the Valley, near Hollywood. This man was attracted to him because of the magnetic bond between them; the mutal love of animals. He told this man of a small ranch for rent or sale, near his dog training school. When he went to look at it with his wife, he knew instantly that this was the answer to his needs. He had some savings, so he put down two months rent in advance and signed a five year lease. He fixed up his own kennels, for he was skillful with tools, and began by boarding people's pets. Within six months time he had enough money to buy some highly pedigreed stock and he began breeding and showing his wonderful dogs. In another year's time he was winning first prizes at dog shows and he became famous for his fine pedigreed stock. He was successful because he loved his work, and he lavished affection and kindness on all his pets. He told me that every time he sold one of his fine dogs he suffered keenly, so much did he love them.

Cosmic power to make a fortune flows to your higher mind centers when you fill your mind with cosmic capacitators. These are positive desires to improve yourself, to help the world, and to make a fortune for the good of others.

These cosmic capacitators can be programmed into your higher mind centers every day through a simple process: Each day set a goal for yourself that is easy to achieve.

When you have achieved these small goals, you will have more confidence in yourself, so set a goal that is a step higher than the others that motivated you.

For instance, you can ask cosmic mind to give you a trip to Europe or any other place you choose. Ask for the sum of two thousand dollars from an unexpected source. Each day affirm that this money will come to you and that you will make your trip.

Get travel literature from an agency, graphically picturing the places you want to visit. Program these photographs in your conscious, subconscious and superconscious minds each day. Soon, without much effort on your part, the money will come for you to take the projected trip—or to achieve any other goal where money is required.

How One Lady Attracted a Trip to Italy Through This Method

Last year, while I was visiting Venice, Italy, I ran into a lecture member from New York, who had studied these principles in my classes. She was startled to meet me there, and told me excitedly:

"You programmed this trip into my consciousness one night at class when you told of the beauty of Italy. I asked cosmic mind to bring me the money to visit Rome, Florence, Milan and

Venice. It came about in the most unexpected way. A member of our family I had never seen in Minneapolis had an estate that was being settled, and I was mentioned in the will and received three thousand dollars! I had never met the distant relative in my life."

God works in a mysterious way, His wonders to perform. We must set into motion the cosmic forces through the cosmic capacitators that we program into our higher minds.

These cosmic capacitators can be for good health, money, success in a business, romantic and marriage fulfillment; anything you desire can be given to this higher mind and it will set the psychic machinery into motion that makes your dreams come true.

Cosmic Power Motivator Number Four

Set the Psychic Thermostat in Your Mind
to Success not Failure

You possess a biological thermostat which is constantly set at approximately ninety-eight degrees for your body's comfort. No matter what outer weather conditions prevail, this thermostat is always adjusting your body to the atmosphere.

Likewise you may set the Psychic Thermostat of your higher mind to any degree of success you choose.

Most people set this Psychic Thermostat to failure, not success. They are driven by a compulsion to fail, and seldom achieve any real, outstanding success. They make the excuses that the rich have all the money; that they lack education, that their parents were poor; that one must be crooked and dishonest to be rich. These thoughts set the thermostat of the higher psychic centers on failure not success and they cannot succeed until they change the Psychic Thermostat from negative to positive.

He Set His Psychic Thermostat to Failure

A man I once knew constantly lamented the fact that life had passed him by and never given him a thing without hard work.

He never had enough money for the extra little luxuries he wanted for his family. He had early set his Psychic Thermostat to failure by the fact he was brought up by poor farmers in upstate New York, and he had heard his mother and father talk about the hard life of a farmer, until he was conditioned to believe all his life he would be poor.

When he moved to the city and went to work as a carpenter, he carried this psychic conditioning with him. He had two children, a wife who had the same negative outlook on life, and his life was one of bickering, confusion, and failure. He never did know how to change his consciousness from the psychic motivator of failure to that of success. He will always remain a failure unless he learns of this tremendous secret force which can transform him.

How One Man Achieved Outstanding Success Through This Plan

Another man I know, who studied these cosmic secrets with me in California, set his thermostat psychically for outstanding success in the real estate business. He was guided to take a course in real estate from an evening school. He obtained a license and began a new career at thirty-five years of age. He used psychic motivators to give him an energy boost every day before he began work, and many times during the day when he needed extra stimulation. He would affirm quietly:

> I know that today will be one of my best days to make sales. I charge my mind now with the motivating force of success. I will give value to every person I sell. I will be honest, and tell my clients the truth, even when it may hurt my sale. I recognize the divine law of increase and invoke that law in all my business affairs. I now sow the seeds of success, service, good and truth, and these will reap the cosmic crop of prosperity and riches.

This man stopped at least ten times a day and gave himself this cosmic treatment. His brain centers were fed the positive psychic capacitators which began to show immediate results in big sales. He later invested in land near a town called Lancaster, and now ten years later, he is a millionaire!

Cosmic Motivator Number Five

The Cosmic Urge to Love, Marry and Have a Family

This is one of the greatest of all cosmic motivators, for it expresses the basic instinct in the human psyche. Man was not created to live alone; he was born to know his true soul mate and to unite in the glorious bonds of matrimony and raise a wonderful family. This procreative urge is strong in all normal human beings and must be expressed as a cosmic motivating force.

Express the cosmic force of love every day in your life by loving the world and all people. Try to see through human weaknesses and forgive people for their shortcomings.

Find your true soul mate by holding in consciousness the ideals that you want in your future husband or wife. Project these ideals in your own personality and soon you will magnetize the one person who is best suited to you for love and marriage.

How This Cosmic Secret Force Brought a Woman
Her True Soul Mate

Nora H. was a failure in love and marriage. She told me this in my first interview with her. She was then thirty years old and had already been married and divorced twice. She knew something was wrong, but she didn't know what.

I soon discovered that Nora was using the emotion of love merely for self-gratification, to satisfy some deep emotional need, but she was giving nothing to the union. Each husband left her because she did not make him happy. She had two children by her first marriage, and these children were given to her by the court, but they were denied a father's love. Her second husband did not like her children for they reflected the same personality as their mother. They were demanding, selfish, quarrelsome and spiteful.

I told Nora H. after analyzing her, "You must open the portals of your heart and soul to true, unselfish love. You are denying one of life's most priceless privileges to your children;

the right to have the love and protection of a father." Then I gave her the cosmic regime to follow for projecting the ideal qualities that she wanted in a future husband. She began to change her own character from one of nagging, critical, fault-finding, to one of love and consideration. I gave her a cosmic motivator to affirm every day, several times.

> I now project unselfish love. I magnetize the qualities of good, happiness, optimism, selflessness and divine love. I desire a true soul mate who will have these qualities in his personality. I wish to have a beautiful home for my children. I shall give of my love unstintingly and joyously share my life with my true spiritual mate.

The cosmic power that this woman invoked truly worked a miracle in a span of three months. She had occasion to see an attorney regarding the matter of her last divorce and settlement. The young attorney she went to was a thirty-five year old bachelor, and she later told me that something electric seemed to go between them on that first meeting. After subsequent meetings she found that this young man had never married because he could not find a woman with the traits of character he wanted in a wife. Within three months time this attorney proposed marriage to her and they were married. He loved his ready-made family, and they adored their new father. This marriage has now been successful for three years, and I believe it will continue indefinitely.

SUMMARY OF CHAPTER THREE

1. The spiritual protoplasm that fills the invisible interstices of the cosmos and how to tap it through Mind Cosmology.
2. How to create thought forms to shape the invisible protoplasm into the pictures of things you want to materialize in your life.
3. How to use cosmic power motivators to bring you riches and fulfill your every dream in life.
4. How the ego-drive to achieve your life goal can bring you amazing cosmic mind power to fulfill your destiny in life.

5. How one woman was inspired to achieve greatness through releasing her creative power under the impetus of the ego-drive.
6. The five simple steps you may take to achieve ego-drive and attain any goal in life that you consciously choose.
7. How an insurance salesman used cosmic ego-drive to achieve an increase of one hundred percent in his sales.
8. The secret formula for building a fortune through the science of Mind Cosmology.
9. How you may set the Psychic Thermostat of your higher mind for the achievement of any amount of money you desire.
10. One man in California became a millionaire by setting his Psychic Thermostat on achieving fortune through real estate.
11. The cosmic motivator of true love and how it can bring you your true soul mate and permanent happiness in love and marriage.
12. How this cosmic secret power brought one woman her true soul mate after being divorced two times and having failed in marriage.

The Five Mystic Laws of Mind
Cosmology That Solve Problems
and Bring Good Luck

Mind Cosmology works its miracles through definite, well-established cosmic laws that rule the entire universe.

When you have unsolvable problems that refuse to yield to any known power, you may tap a stratum of cosmic mind which knows the answers and can immediately solve the problem.

When you persistently have bad luck, you can tap this same power of cosmic mind to bring you a cycle of good luck.

The five mystic laws that control you and release the magic power of mind cosmology work under the same principle as the law of mathematics. Two and two make four, never five or six. When you live under these laws of mind cosmology you will always get the right results in your life. Nothing will come too late or too early, but every event will follow the cosmic timetable of cycles and bring you creative gifts for every season of your life.

This Woman Lived in a Cloud of Confusion and Bad Luck

One woman I know who had no idea she was creating her own bad luck, lived in a constant cloud of confusion and discord. She was a saleslady in a big department store, but she was soon discharged because she argued with the customers and had constant friction with her co-workers.

This woman's family, two sons and a daughter, had long since lost respect for their mother. The father had deserted them when they were young because of the mother's sharp tongue and constant abuse. She was jealous and suspicious and constantly accused her husband of having an affair with another woman. Finally he was fed up and simply disappeared.

When this woman came into the study of Mind Cosmology she was already in her late forties and told me a long tale of woe about how ungrateful everyone was; what a monster her husband had been; how unfair they were at her place of business. She could not realize that she was creating her own problems and bad luck by her wrong mental attitude.

It took me four weeks, with an interview each week, to set this woman on the right track. I gave her a regime to work on. She was to be busy changing her mental attitude and stop finding fault with people and the world. I gave her the following cosmology affirmations to affirm every day, as often as she needed them to keep herself mentally in balance.

I now create my own mental atmosphere of good luck. I am not a victim of circumstances. I can change that which I do not like by changing my mind. I now see perfection all around me. I am in tune with people and the laws of life. I radiate poise, confidence and love. I know that all my problems are now overcome through my understanding of others, through patience and good-will. I am joyous and expectant of my good.

The next four weeks of living under this mind cosmology regime did wonders for this woman. She actually became a new person! Her facial expression changed. She had formerly looked cross and the corners of her mouth drooped in perpetual disapproval. She now smiled warmly when she met people. She got another job in a big department store and within three months she was elevated to a position as manager of her department. She later told me, "I can never believe the miracle that has happened to me. Now my children seem to love me more than ever, and I have met a man who wants to marry me, if I can get a divorce."

How to Use the Five Mystic Laws of Mind Cosmology That Solve Problems and Bring Good Luck

Law One.   Positive Identification with the Creative Power in the Universe.

Begin this moment to identify yourself with the creative power that rules the universe. Each day acknowledge that God is the supreme Power back of the universe and that you align yourself with Him and His divine laws. These laws are love and good. When you are good you will cease to be troubled by problems. These life experiences we call problems exist for all people; but you will meet these challenges with new courage and energy when you operate under the cosmic laws of good and love.

Positive identification with the creative power of the cosmos gives you a sense of being aware, of being one with the power. This mystic law in Mind Cosmology is known as the I Am Consciousness.

At least ten times a day affirm these laws of cosmic identity:

I am one with cosmic power and can solve all problems.
I am joyous and my problems now dissolve under the rays of God's infinite intelligence, love and joy.
I am prosperous and achieve riches mentally, physically, materially and spiritually.
I am healthy and every cell of my body radiates life energy, youth and long life.
I am in the magic circle of God's Divine Love and attract my true soul mate and radiant happiness in love and marriage.

How She Overcame Tremendous Problems in Her Work

A young girl worked in a law firm and she disliked her work because it was so confining. There was discord and friction in her office which she carried home with her. As she lived with her mother and father, she felt further suppressed and stifled by her inability to overcome her perplexing problems. She felt limited, since she knew she should be in creative work that she enjoyed, such as commercial art, interior decorating or advertising.

This young lady came to a lecture series I gave in New York. She learned how the laws of Mind Cosmology work, and she began to apply them to her life.

Instead of being bored with her work and desiring change, she stopped wasting her mental energy on regrets, dissatisfaction and discontent with her lot in life. I gave her a new regime to work on. I told her to enroll in a fashion designing course at a famous school of design. She took a night course and soon was so busy meeting artistic people and doing work she loved that she forgot her discontent and frustration.

Within a year this girl graduated with honors from this school. She was given a position with one of the leading department stores in designing their new fashions. Soon she was travelling to Paris, London, Rome, searching for new ideas for her firm and making more money than she had ever dreamed was possible!

Law Two.   Desire for Cosmic Knowledge and Psychic
                  Guidance

This cosmic law works in all creation. An acorn has an innate desire to become an oak tree, not a maple tree or a pumpkin. When it expresses this cosmic urge, it is able to attract to itself all the elements to make a perfect oak tree. It does not become a maple tree or a pumpkin because this was not the psychic guidance it received from all-knowing, cosmic mind.

Let the guiding light of your life be to accumulate cosmic knowledge and to open the higher psychic centers where you will receive psychic guidance.

Become a mental and psychic giant!

You have the power to become anything you wish once you tap this higher psychic power within. It knows how to solve your problems, how to bring you good luck, how to make you successful and rich, healthy and happy.

Each day when you start your work, ask this higher cosmic mind to guide you in your every move. When you have a complex problem to solve and do not know which way to turn, go into the silence for a moment by saying quietly, "Peace, be still. Be still and know that I am God."

Then wait for a moment until you are completely still. Suddenly your mind will receive promptings from the higher psychic mind and you will then forget your problem. Go about your regular affairs and suddenly you will be inspired to do the very thing that solves the problem perfectly.

How a Man Was Able to Win a Law Suit by Psychic Guidance

A man I once knew started a lawsuit for one hundred and fifty thousand dollars. The attorneys told him he could not possibly win, for the other side had powerful forces in politics that would make him lose the case. The man had studied Mind Cosmology in my classes and knew the power of his higher psychic mind. He realized that he would be told the right things to say when his time came on the witness stand.

His two attorneys were confused and upset, but this man maintained his inner calm and kept affirming:

> I am under control of my higher mind. I am calm and still.
> Divine justice will now triumph in my life. I ask psychic
> guidance as to what I shall say and do on the witness stand.

When he got up to testify he said a tremendous feeling of calmness came over him. He depended entirely on his higher psychic mind to give him the words with which to answer the questioning attorney. No matter how the opposition attorney tried to confuse him, he kept affirming to himself: "Divine Justice will prevail. My mind is now calm and under perfect control."

He and his attorney were both surprised at how he answered each question on the witness stand. When he got down he knew within himself that he had won his case.

The jury was out only half an hour when they returned with a verdict giving him his victory and one hundred and fifty thousand dollars!

Law Three. Expand Your Consciousness to Encompass the Power of the Master Mind of the Universe

Everywhere in nature we see the master mind of the universe doing its miraculous work.

This master mind works through three forces:

Omniscience—All-knowing, all-wise.
Omnipotence—All-powerful, all-encompassing.
Omnipresence—Everywhere present at all times.

This cosmic mind works in the soil, in the air, in the seas, and also within your mind and body. To achieve omniscience expand your consciousness to encompass all branches of knowledge. Study a little about psychology, philosophy, industry, art, music, business and finance, travel and foreign countries, literature, poetry, astronomy and biology. As the centers of your consciousness absorb more knowledge, you will achieve the state of omniscience, where cosmic mind can pour its intellectual treasures into your brain centers.

How a Mother Used Omniscience to Know
   How to Help Her Child

A woman I once knew had some training in the science of Mind Cosmology. She had a five-year-old son who was suddenly very sick. The doctors could not find out what was wrong with him and he became weaker and weaker every day. The mother was desperate for she knew the child would die if she could not find out what to do.

She withdrew her mind from the problem and went into the silence, using prayer as the connecting link between her mind and the omniscient mind of God. She asked for guidance as to what she should do to heal her son. The boy was then in a state where he frequently went into a coma and then later came out of it. The mother sat beside her child's bed waiting for him to awaken, when suddenly something within her said, "Give your boy orange juice—lots of orange juice."

She left someone to watch her child while she went to the market and bought oranges. She returned and squeezed some orange juice and when her son awakened, she gave him two glasses of it. After the orange juice the boy seemed to be somewhat better, and did not slip back into the usual coma. Then something within the mother told her to go and squeeze more oranges and give the juice to the boy. She did, and he eagerly drank the orange juice, until within two hours time she had given him four glasses of orange juice. The boy started to improve from that moment on; the next two days she gave him the juice from ten to fifteen oranges a day, and within that time the boy responded so beautifully that he wanted to go out into the yard to play!

The mother was afraid to let him go out, so she called another doctor and asked him to come and examine her son. When the doctor came and examined him, he said, "Why, there's nothing wrong with this boy."

The mother then told him how dangerously ill he had been and how she had given the boy orange juice and how he had recovered. The doctor then told her that her son had been suffering from a sever case of acidosis and the orange juice or other citrus fruits would have an almost miraculous effect in healing him. The mother had been intuitively guided to do the right thing for her boy and he lived and became strong and healthy.

How to Use Omnipotence

Each day affirm that you are drawing on the cosmic power of the God-mind. Know that it is omnipotent, all-powerful, all-encompassing, with the ability to solve your every problem.

Affirm several times a day: "I draw on the omnipotence of

cosmic mind and my problems now dissolve. I am all-powerful, and my mind and body are fortified by the inner strength of divine mind."

How a Man Used This Cosmic Force for Changing His Life

A man who came to some of my lectures on Cosmology, had a tremendous problem which he could not solve by himself. He came to me for guidance and I told him he must look for help from the higher God-mind within his own mind that would give him the strength to overcome the thing troubling him. He had a son who was only eighteen years of age and had taken to drinking. While drunk one night he had driven a car without a license and killed an old man who was crossing the street. This terrible tragedy blighted this man's entire life, as it was his only child. He and his wife were tragic-stricken and came to me for guidance. The boy was free on bail and his trial would soon come up. I told this man to draw on the cosmic mind power, and utilize the cosmic force of omnipotence. He, himself could do little for his son, but God, who knows all and is all, could help him. Under the law of divine justice, I told him, he could ask for his son to be freed and not to be sent to prison for a year or two, as was likely under the laws governing manslaughter. The fact the young man had been drinking made it a much more serious offense.

When the day of the trial came up, the father was mentally in a state of calmness and expectation that his son would be freed by the jury. When all the testimony had been heard the jury retired for deliberation. During that period the father kept repeating positive affirmations that all would be well, and that his son would be free. The jury deliberated for three hours, and when they returned their verdict was "Guilty of manslaughter in the first degree."

Even with the weight of this negative evidence the father did not give up hope. He knew that his son was to be free. When the judge sentenced the boy, he said, "Your conscience will punish you more than this court ever can. I thereby sentence you to one year in prison, with the sentence suspended on condition that you report for probation every month, and on further condition that you remain sober and do not drive a car for one year."

This was, in the father's opinion, a just sentence, and his boy was remanded in his custody. Since that day his son has been sober, studious and changed in character. He learned his cosmic lesson and will probably never err again in the same respect.

How the Force of Omnipresence Works in Cosmology

Omnipresence affirms the reality of the cosmic mind in all elements of creation. We marvel at the fact that the entire universe runs with such perfect order and regularity. The stars rise and set; the moon and earth revolve around the sun; the seasons come and go in regular cycles that are predictable. The cosmic mind is like a guardian angel, always supervising, always knowing and caring for its loving children.

You are never isolated and alone. You can tap this cosmic mind to solve all problems, to guide you to your right work, to make more money, to seek out your right destiny. Wherever you are this omnipresent cosmic intelligence is already working out your destiny if you but know it and have faith in this higher power.

How a Man Was Guided by This Power in South America

A man who had been to some of my lectures in New York, had a deep, inner urge to go to South America. He wrote me a letter a short time after he arrived telling me an amazing story. When he got to the location he had chosen he found he did not speak the language, which was Portuguese, he had no contacts or friends, he had very little money, but he began to affirm his power of omnipresence. He knew that this cosmic mind power was there in Brazil, as much as it had been in New York, or in his native land of Greece, which he had left to make his fortune.

He quietly affirmed that he would be led to his right work. He expected his good to come from wherever he was. He relaxed and went about the business of settling in his new home with his wife and son.

One day he had an impulse to go into a restaurant that was run by a countryman of his and who had been in Brazil for ten years. They talked for a short time and this man told him, "I have a friend who has some capital and he's looking for a partner to go into his big importing and exporting business. Why don't you go and see him."

The man went and instantly knew that this was going to be his big business opportunity. The other man was a native of Brazil, but spoke Greek, having worked with people of that nationality. He told this man he needed a good partner in his business and would take only a few thousand dollars, as down payment, the balance to be paid off from profits of the business.

The two men signed legal papers and my friend was in business. He told me in his letter that from the moment he went into the business he knew he would make a fortune. Now they are handling so much business that they must expand their offices and warehouses!

Law Four.   Tap the Divine Law of Cosmic Abundance and Use It on Every Plane

Everywhere you look in nature there is abundance. Poverty is man-made! Your problems are also created by this limited, human consciousness. When you expand the horizons of your mind to encompass the cosmic realms you realize that you have limited yourself and that is why you may be suffering from lack, limitation, poverty and insecurity.

Each day affirm as you start your day, "I know that today I shall be able to attract my good. Abundance is all about me. I now receive divine inspiration to do my work and achieve my destiny."

This Positive Law of Abundance Brought Riches to a Woman

A woman had lived all her life in the shadow of poverty. She had three children—eight, ten, and thirteen years of age. Her husband had died in an industrial accident, and she had only his small insurance, and a tremendous desire to provide for her children. She casually came to one of my lectures on Mind Cosmology with a friend, who had received help. She listened to the lecture and then went home and began to practice the principles she had heard.

She sat in meditation for an hour every day asking cosmic mind to show her what to do. One day, she received an impulse from cosmic mind to read a newspaper and look in the business opportunities section. There she saw an ad asking for someone with small capital to go into a perfume business with him. The woman had an urge to write the man and after she had an interview with him, she found that he needed the exact amount of her insurance money. He had formulas for perfume, as he was a chemist, but it was a different type of perfume; it was based on the astrological signs of the zodiac!

This woman asked cosmic mind if she should trust this man, and the answer came through in the positive. She withdrew her three thousand dollars from the bank, gave it to the man, and he signed papers making her an equal partner. Within three months time they had distributors working in the Eastern states placing their product in many drug stores and novelty shops. Soon they had expanded their business to such a point that she drew from the business the entire amount she had advanced and was receiving each month more money than she had ever had before. The business is still growing and expanding, and this woman says she knows she had guidance from cosmic mind.

Law Five.   Enlist the Aid of Your Subconscious Mind to Achieve Power to Solve Problems and Bring You Luck

Your subconscious mind is a very important aid to your life. It heals your body, it keeps your heart beating and causes you to breathe; it digests your food, and takes care of all the automatic functions of the body and mind. Your memory, imagination and visualization come under its control.

Sit every day and ask this subconscious mind how to solve problems. Ask it for guidance as to how to increase your income; tell it every night of the miracles you want it to perform and it will act for you under definite cosmic laws.

How Business Problems Were Solved for This Man
 Through His Subconscious

A man I once knew had many business worries. He was in a real estate development project where he stood to lose all his money if he did not sell his holdings. It was not a time when real estate was selling well however, and he could not sell. He tried subdividing the land but without success.

He went into subconscious meditation and asked his higher mind to help him solve his problem. As he sat quietly waiting for the answer, something seemed to tell him, "Why don't you advertise that you are going to open a big health community in your area. Give a lecture and invite people to attend and then tell them about the benefits of buying your land."

This idea was so startling that the man could hardly believe it would work. He put an ad in the papers telling about his plan to open a big health community with recreational facilities, swimming pool, community playgrounds and other benefits and he invited people to come to a lecture he was giving that week-end. The hall he had rented was packed, and people were vitally interested in sharing his community to get away from the polluted air of New York, so he engaged a big bus and drove people to his community in nearby Pennsylvannia. There he had salesmen ready to show his land to potential customers, and soon he had sold every available lot and could have sold fifty more, if he had had them!

The community he had planned began to take shape and is now a thriving, health-minded, progressive center with its own schools, churches, recreation park and community pool. This man made a fortune, and also benefitted the community he helped to establish.

SUMMARY OF CHAPTER FOUR

1. How to contact the cosmic mind that helps solve problems and which can guide you to your true destiny.
2. How one woman overcame her problems by using Mind Cosmology to bring her good luck and prosperity.

3. The five Mystic Laws of Mind Cosmology that bring good luck and help overcome problems.

4. Law One: How to achieve positive identification with the creative power that rules the universe and build the I Am consciousness.

5. How one young woman got out of office work and became a top notch designer in one years time, travelling all over the world.

6. Law Two: The desire for cosmic knowledge and cosmic guidance and how it can make anyone a mental and psychic giant.

7. One man used this law to win a court case for one hundred and fifty thousand dollars.

8. Law Three: Expand your consciousness to encompass the power of the master mind of the universe.

9. The powerful forces released through omniscience, omnipotence, and omnipresence, and how to use them to solve problems and achieve good luck.

10. How a desperate mother saved her child's life through the great cosmic law of omniscience, which told her what to do when all doctors had failed to save her boy.

11. How one man used the cosmic law of omnipotence to help solve his son's problem, when the boy killed a man with his car.

12. How one man was guided to live in Brazil and go into a successful business through the cosmic law of omnipresence.

13. Law Four: Tap the divine law of cosmic abundance and use it on every plane.

14. How this positive law of abundance brought one woman riches.

15. Law Five: Enlist the aid of your subconscious mind to achieve power to solve problems and bring you good luck.

16. How one man solved his problem of disposing of large land holdings for a fortune, through using the subconscious mind to guide him to the right action.

5

The Cosmic Plan for
Your Personal
Achievement

There is a cosmic blue print of destiny that has been created by divine intelligence for every living thing on this planet. This includes the highest form of creation, man. When you once know this divine plan for personal achievement and greatness you will be able to use the principles of mind cosmology to mold and shape a brilliant destiny for yourself.

You were created to know a unique and brilliant destiny, for you are different from all the other three billion people on this earth. This diversity of gifts and talents is seen in all nature. Cosmic mind has created a vast variety of species of trees, vegetables, flowers, fruit, and animals. Each has its own distinct character and function and no two forms of creation are ever alike. No two blades of grass, no two grains of sand possess the same imprint. Think of what a vast intelligence exists in the universe that could create such a diversity of products.

62

Nature is God's experimental workshop for evolving and creating new forms of life. This process of creation is ever-expanding and never-ending. It works in nature under cosmic laws, and it also works in your life to bring you to a greater state of perfection.

In this chapter you will learn how to use the cosmic plan that is programmed into your mind, body and soul, for your own personal achievement and future greatness.

The Six Cosmic Creative Urges You Can Use for Yourself

There are six basic cosmic creative urges in Mind Cosmology, which you can use to shape your own future destiny. When you apply these urges to your own life you will be amazed at how you will have the power to create any destiny you choose.

1. The Hunger Urge

This comes first in man's basic urges, for the body must be fed correctly to give it strength and power to meet life's challenges.

In an experiment with rats in a maze, it was found that rats that were well-fed and secure learned how to solve problems and get through a maze faster than those that were hungry and desperate.

Use this natural hunger urge to give you an incentive to better health, more energy and greater productivity. Do not let it degenerate into faulty diet habits, gluttony or carelessness in your care of the body. The body works like a machine, it functions under your subconscious mind and can work perfectly to give you bodily health, vigor and youth. Only when it is allowed to fall into wrong eating habits does the body become obese, sick and malfunctioning.

The hunger urge gives you the basic cosmic desire for self-preservation. The will to live must be strongly implemented. Each day affirm your laws for the body's survival and health.

Say positive affirmations to your subconscious mind to help you achieve a healthy, strong, vital body as follows:

> I am healthy. I now project the urge of self-preservation. My subconscious mind will now direct me to the right health habits. I now follow my intuitive mind as to the right diet. I imprint on the cells of my body the mental picture of health. I will live to be one hundred years of age or more, functioning in perfect health, with all my faculties.

How to Build the Health Habit in Your Mind and Body

A. Each day when you get up decide you will think only of good health all day, and not get into the habit of thinking of sickness, age and debility.

B. Avoid using negative words all day, such as old, sick, hospital, accident, death, fear, worry, hate, anxiety, heart trouble, or the names of other diseases. This will help clear your subconscious mind of all negative debris each day and fill it with only life-giving, healthy thoughts.

C. When anyone asks you how you feel, always reply, "I feel great." Soon the habit of thinking you feel great will affect your body cells, for they reflect what you think. A chain reaction is set into motion between your brain cells and your body cells and you will soon reflect better health and more youthful energy.

D. Adopt the health habit of being conscious of your breathing at least five to ten times a day, breathing deeply and hold the breath a count or two before releasing it. This helps charge the bloodstream with fresh oxygen, magnetism and electricity which are vital to your body's good health.

E. When you eat food be aware that it is life and energy. Take as many vegetables and fruits as possible to counteract the heavy intake of carbohydrates and meat proteins. Learn the correct amounts of food your body requires and be aware of a balanced diet, with the proper minerals and vitamins you need.

F. Refuse to fill your body with chemicals that might poison you such as nicotine, alcohol, caffeine and artificial foods that might harm your body. Most medicines, even aspirin, should be avoided and used only under a physician's prescription.

2. The Sex Urge

This is the drive that motivates people to achievement of great things when it is correctly channeled.

It is vitally important to build the emotion of love into a daily uplifting experience, for love is the ultimate expression of the sex urge between members of the opposite sex.

Back of all creation is this urge to love and be loved. You can direct your sex energies into creative channels. Find someone you can love and concentrate your creative powers on this divine emotion and it will soon change your life.

How an Artist Used This Creative Emotion to Paint

George G. was an artist who painted drab, uncolorful pictures which did not sell. When he came into our work in New York City, and showed me photos of some of his works, I realized that he lacked the inspiration that an artist needs. He was twenty-five years of age and lived alone in Greenwich Village. He had no one he loved and no special reason for being an artist, except something told him he must paint in order to be happy.

I told him the basic need for love for all creative artists and advised him to go out and fall in love with someone with whom he could share his desire for creating beauty. He began going to the Art Student's League in Manhattan, and there he met a very beautiful model with whom he fell in love. Within a month's time George returned with some of his canvasses and I was truly amazed to see the difference in his work! Most of his paintings were of Jane, the girl he had fallen in love with, and they showed tremendous promise that he at last was on the road to becoming a great artist.

3. The Money Urge

Making a success in life, being rich, and having money is one of the basic urges that drives most of humanity to great goal-achievement.

Money, in itself, is not a goal worth striving for, but the desire to make money to do something good and constructive with, has always been an incentive that has led to some of the world's greatest achievements in business and industry.

How to Build the Success Habit

1. Have a goal that you want to achieve, which includes others. A desire to have money to educate your children, to buy a home, to have cultural benefits, to help the world, to establish a foundation for orphans or other underprivileged people—these are all good cosmic motives for achieving riches.

2. Fill your mind with success thoughts each day. Tell yourself that you will succeed. Use positive affirmations. Stand before your mirror each morning and look at yourself, thinking of yourself as having something of value that you will give the world that day. Then say the positive affirmations that will program success into your subconscious mind as follows:

> I will succeed. I will become successful and rich. I desire money so I may help my family live a better life. I desire fame and fortune so I can help the world. I see money as being good, not evil. I know there is abundance in the world for all creation and I now accept my abundance from cosmic mind.

3. Success and money-making ability depend a great deal on the self-image you have created for the world to see. You must think big, feel and look important, speak in an authoritative manner. You are a salesman in life selling yourself, and if you do not have faith in yourself or your product, the world will not give you riches. Cultivate the self-image of success. Read periodicals such as *Fortune, Forbes,* and *The Wall Street Journal,* which deal with big business and magnetize your brain centers with the ideas that have made men rich.

4. Get in the habit of thinking in terms of big money. To cultivate this habit write down on a piece of paper the sum of $1,000, and concentrate on achieving this amount. Then after a

few days, write down $10,000, and concentrate on this amount; gradually increase the figures to $100,000, and then to $1,000,000 until your consciousness expands to a point where you can imagine yourself having the amounts of money you desire.

4. The Mental and Intellectual Urge

You have been given a desire to add to your mental and intellectual gifts, so you may enjoy life more fully. This instinct in the human psyche has led to our great inventions, discoveries, scientific achievements, and industrial triumphs. Man's desire to know the cosmic forces that keep our earth spinning around the sun led him to invent the space ships that took us to the moon on a glorious adventure in time and space and returned us back to earth again, immeasurably enriched.

Someone has said, "Ignorance is the only sin." You can only overcome ignorance with the cosmic light of truth.

How to Build Your Intellectual Powers

1. Give yourself a self-study program which includes at least a full hour of reading good books each day. Avoid putting into your mind most of the negative books that are published, and concentrate on studying self-improvement books that can help you really improve your mind.

2. If you lack a college education, this need not be a hindrance in achieving a great destiny. Many of our greatest geniuses did not go to college and some did not even go to school. You can improve your mind by taking evening courses in high school, or through correspondence. Public libraries are filled with wonderful books that can add to your intellectual treasures. Keep studying and evolving your mind throughout your entire life, for as you expand your consciousness you will expand the horizons of your world and accomplish more.

3. Acquire a little knowledge about many things. Study a little psychology, philosophy, science, astronomy, biology,

geology, and sociology. Know the world in which you live. Be conversant about world events and expand your interests to other people and other countries.

How a Woman Travelled Around the World by Expanding Her Intellectual Horizons

A very interesting example of how you can benefit from expanding the horizons of your mind, was that of a lecture member in New York, who studied these principles in my classes. She was forty-five years of age and a widow, with no future except to wait for the onset of lonely old age. She told me this in her first interview with me.

I gave this woman a mental program to work on in which she was to take up something she enjoyed doing in some evening high school. She came back and told me that she had decided on fashion photography, a most unusual and interesting field.

She enrolled in a school of fashion photography, graduated a year later, with her mind now set on a new career. She was guided, she told me later, by her psychic mind, to a party where she met the fashion editor of one of America's leading magazines. The editor found her fascinating, for they both talked the same language—fashion. One of the magazine's big photographers was going on an assignment to the leading capitals of Europe and needed an assistant. This woman got the job and it led her to London, Paris, Rome, Berlin, and other fascinating cities in Europe. She could never have achieved this high goal if she had not first prepared her mind with accurate knowledge in the fields of fashion and photography.

5. The Urge for Social Acceptance

Strong in the natural urges that you have within your mind is the need for social acceptance. You need to belong to people, and you must have friends, companionship and understanding relationships with others. If you do not have this expression of your natural urge, you will live a life of loneliness and heartache.

1. Remember the magnetic law of attraction which we invoke in our study of Mind Cosmology; you attract what you think and what you are. Involve in the centers of your consciousness thoughts of friendship and reciprocity. Be friendly, smile at people, share your happy experiences with them, be considerate and thoughtful of them, remember their birthdates, their anniversaries and special events. They will respond with friendship and love. Remember Emerson's injunction: "To have a friend, be a friend."

2. Cultivate hobbies and avocations that take you into groups where other people with similar interests meet. These can be class groups in art, music, dancing, drama, ceramics, short-story writing, or foreign language studies. A good place to seek out such groups is in the evening high schools they have in most cities. Other places are in church groups and community centers.

A woman from our lecture group in California took this advice when she told me she was lonely and had no friends. She was thirty-five years of age, and unmarried. She wanted friends and hoped that she might meet some man who would fall in love with her and marry her, but she lived with a crippled mother, never had friends at the house and had no opportunity to meet people.

She joined a ceramics study class two nights a week. There she met people who were also interested in her hobby, and out of that group she attracted a retired businessman who became her closest friend. Two months later she had a proposal of marriage from him and the last I knew they were planning to get married. By starting the creative flow of mind power in the direction of social action, this woman was following the natural urge to have friends and be socially acceptable.

3. Cultivate the mental qualities that other people will find interesting. Magnetism flows from a mind that is creatively engaged. Build your interest in the current scene, be conversant with the latest news events; know about the latest things going on in the world of art, music, and the theater; read book reviews giving opinions about current literature. As you cultivate your

mind centers you will radiate more magnetism, but, more importantly, you will have interesting material to talk about when you meet people at social gatherings.

6. The Spiritual Urge for Soul Fulfillment

Within every human being there is an inherent desire to know God and worship Him. As Mind Cosmology relates to the totality of consciousness, and not to mind power alone, it is essential that man be in daily communication with the highest spiritual power in the universe. Only then does he find that ultimate fulfillment, which mystics of the Far East call Darshan.

1. Begin each day with a prayer of thanksgiving for the gift of life, and dedicate your mind, body and soul to God in His service and for the good of humanity.

2. Several times during the day stop and appreciate the universe that God created for your enjoyment. Give silent thanks for the beauty of nature; express gratitude for the good things you enjoy every day; thank God for the food you eat, for the joyous relationships you have with your family and friends. As you express gratitude for these things higher power begins to flow through your mind and body centers, giving you greater joy and contentment.

3. Absorb beauty and goodness, for the soul thrives on these two attributes of the Divine Image we call God. Every day of your life strive to search for beauty all about you; see the best in people, and when you observe some ugly trait in others, treat them with the spiritual plus of beauty. When someone is unkind, or does some act that is not good, treat him with the spiritual plus of goodness. The Bible defines God as being good, and when you enthrone goodness, you will automatically program your higher mind to good thoughts, good words and good deeds, and you will experience good from the world.

4. Live in the spiritual aura of love, kindness and gentility. The soul in all its purity knows only love, for it was created in the spiritual love of God and sent forth on its mystical journey

through time and space to express this divine emotion. The Bible also defines God as Love, and when you perform loving deeds and hold love in your heart and soul for the entire world, and love God more than you love life, you will be elevated to the highest pinnacles of personal achievement.

How Spiritual Love Changes Life

A sixty-year-old woman, whose husband had died, felt that she had no reason for living. She learned in our lectures how important the emotion of love is throughout our entire lives, if one has someone to live for. She retired to a home for elderly people and wondered how she could express the divine emotion of love there. I told her to look around in her own environment and find people who were less fortunate than herself and do some kindly service for them. Soon she was busy reading for elderly women who had poor eyesight, writing letters for those too feeble to do so, and in other ways helping others find happiness. She became so involved in expressing love that her own health improved and she was happier than she had been in many years.

An actress I once knew in Hollywood had this problem: she was disliked by all the publicity people because of her haughty airs and arrogance. She was called hard-hearted and cold, but I knew she had a good heart and really wanted to love and be loved. Her attitude was a defense mechanism from an early childhood of misery and lack of love. I told her the secret of using the spiritual emotion of love and expressing it to everyone who worked with her, and soon this star became the most beloved person in Hollywood. She is now more famous than when she was younger, and the press gives her nothing but praise.

5. Concentrate each day, for at least a half hour a day, on your own spiritual growth and evolement. Study the spiritual laws given in the Bible, such as the Ten Commandments, the Sermon on the Mount, and the other great spiritual laws that show you how to live and express God's Divine Presence in your daily life.

6. Memorize the 23rd Psalm and the 91st Psalm and whenever you are in need of spiritual help or guidance, turn to these two powerful statements of your protection and security. Repeat them whenever you feel upset or unhappy. Say them several times a day until you are absolutely in tune with the spiritual guidance of the cosmic mind that works through your own intuition.

A woman I know who works in public, selling women's articles in a department store, told me she often has disturbing things arise in her work. Customers are often cross and impatient, co-workers sometimes create problems, and when she feels herself at the breaking point she quietly withdraws for a while, and says the 23rd Psalm or the 91st Psalm, and invariably she instantly is restored to her normal state of peace and equilibrium.

Cosmic Enlightenment Comes Through Meditation

To achieve the highest form of spiritual power, you can use the form of transcendental meditation that comes to us from the mysticism of the Far East. Close your eyes and go into a state of reverie where you suspend as much of your conscious mind action as is possible. This is done by concentrating your thoughts on some abstract idea such as beauty, goodness, peace or love. Repeat to yourself some spiritual statement such as this one, from the Bible: "Peace, be still, and know that I am God."

Then when you have achieved perfect stillness within your mind, hold in consciousness the spiritual thought of love. Let your mind dwell on all facets of love, from human love to the love God has for His creation. As you raise your state of vibration from the material to the spiritual plane, you will feel a sense of lightness and inner joy. Your problems will recede into the distance and you will have a feeling of being suspended from all physical activity. You will achieve transcendental meditation in a few moments time as you hold your mind steadily on the abstract thought of love.

Then change the thought to one of peace, and let your mind

encompass all phases of that word, until you are at peace with yourself and with the world.

Then change the thought to good, and dwell on goodness as a divine attribute, reminding yourself that God is good, and that goodness now flows from the celestial heights to the higher centers of your consciousness causing your life to flower with good.

A Concert Pianist Uses This Method
for Achieving Greatness

I know a very famous concert pianist who has used this form of transcendental meditation ever since he learned about it through my lectures in Carnegie Hall. Just before he goes on the stage to play, he sits quietly and meditates on the highest ideals of musical perfection he can visualize. He projects this ideal to his mind, and instructs it to infuse his nerves and muscles with the right degree of tension to produce the harmonious sounds he holds in consciousness. He is invariably calm and self-possessed, and the critics write of the clarity of his tone and the majestic soaring of his music.

SUMMARY OF CHAPTER FIVE

1. How to discover the cosmic blue print of destiny that exists in the universe for you and achieve a brilliant destiny.
2. How to use the six cosmic creative urges to achieve the fulfillment of your every dream.
3. The hunger urge that leads to the body's good health, youth, vitality and long life.
4. How you can build the the health habits in your mind and body that produce vibrant good health and give you vitality and energy.
5. The sex urge and how you can use it to bring you love fulfillment and happiness in love and marriage.
6. How an artist uses this creative emotion to achieve unusual results in his beautiful paintings.

7. How you can use the sex and love urge to create greater happiness in your daily life and bring you untold satisfaction.

8. How you can use the money urge to bring you outstanding success, make you rich, and bring you security.

9. How to build the success habit in your daily life so you will attract money, business opportunities and prosperity.

10. How to cultivate the habit of thinking in terms of success and build a consciousness that can attract to you sums from one thousand to a hundred thousand dollars.

11. Build your mental and intellectual powers to bring you a greater degree of personal achievement in the future.

12. How one woman travelled around the world by using this principle of mind cosmology intellectual expansion.

13. Use the law of mind cosmology to bring you social acceptance and achieve recognition, meet prominent people, and have friends who admire and respect you.

14. How you can use the spiritual urge for achieving soul fulfillment, peace of mind and inner tranquility.

6

How Mind Cosmology Can Help Give You a Healthy Body, Youthful Energy and a Long Life

Mind Cosmology laws exist which can profoundly affect your health and life. You can tap higher wave lengths of thought which are capable of transforming the cells of your brain and body, giving you the control of your body organs and determining your state of health, longevity and youthful vitality.

In the laboratory, the age-old Yoga practices of concentration and meditation have now been tested and amazing discoveries have been made that may well change the course of history, and bring man into an age where mental and physical sickness will end and man will live to be two hundred or more years of age.

In experiments performed at the University of California Medical school and at Stanford University, scientists have now found that man may truly control his body with the power of his mind. When subjects were given experimental tests and wired to electroencephalographs, known as EEG machines, it was found that when a person goes into a deep state of meditation there are profound changes that occur in the brain and body cells.

The person using these powers of the mind could raise or lower his blood pressure at will; he could reduce his body temperature or raise it; he could control the beat of his heart, and vary it as much as five beats per minute!

Scientists found that the brain releases electricity and that there are four primary brain-wave patterns which are named delta, theta, alpha, and beta. Subjects, under meditation, could change the brain wave patterns at will, by thinking certain thoughts and the measureable effects on their bodies showed they guessed correctly four hundred times in a row!

How Fear, Worry and Anxiety May
Completely Disappear

Under these various states of meditation it was found by scientists that fear, worry and anxiety, which often produce physical and mental illness, can be totally eradicated from the human mind.

It was further discovered that people who are heavy smokers were able to overcome the habit. Nineteen narcotics addicts, from the ages of nineteen to twenty-five were completely cured of their habits.

Patients with abnormally high or slow heart rates were able to reduce or accelerate their heart beats at will, causing them to beat at approximately a normal rate of seventy beats per minute.

People who had a compulsion to over-eat and become obese were soon trained to reduce their appetites and were able to achieve normal weight in a short space of time.

By training the mind centers through meditation, it was found that mental awareness was increased, memory was strengthened, and mental and physical efficiency was increased.

Body's Functions Can Be Under Your Control

By using this power of the higher mind and controlling your brain wave patterns, science has now found that you can regulate your own blood pressure, you can increase or decrease the rate of breathing, raise or lower your skin temperature, control the stomach acidity, and digestive processes, and directly control your own muscular activity in any part of your body.

Many of the persons who were used in these scientific experiments had suffered from migraine and other forms of chronic headaches. After a brief period of time in meditation, these headaches completely disappeared! Scientists now believe that eventually tumors may be completely absorbed or cured through the control of the body's blood-flow, under the impetus of a person's higher mind power.

Spiritual and Faith Healing Now Fully Understood

Now, for the first time, science fully understands the mystery behind all spiritual and faith healings.

When you go into a state of spiritual ecstasy, due to faith and prayer, your higher mind sends out magnetic and electrical wave lengths which affect every cell of your brain and body. When you adopt certain states of consciousness, as we shall now learn to do, your mind power extends to your body and its organs, affecting them and imprinting on their sensitive cells, any thought that is registered in your mind.

This amazing mind cosmology discovery had been healing people for over thirty years before science tested its use and its power. In my lecture work in world-famous Carnegie Hall I saw miracle cures of conditions on which doctors had given up.

A woman over sixty years old had an enormous tumor in her abdomen. The doctors were afraid to operate because of her age. She turned to Mind Cosmology for a cure, and began to use the techniques given in this chapter, and within three months time the tumor had been absorbed and was only the size of one's fist. Doctors could not believe the evidence of the x-rays, and in another month of study and meditations, the tumor was reported absorbed!

Sinus, Colds and Bronchial Ailment
Was Healed

Another woman in our lecture group had a tendency to chronic bronchitis, heavy colds, sinus congestion and perpetual headaches that made her life miserable. She would leave New York City in winter to seek relief in warmer climates, but to no avail. She began to practice Mind Cosmology, using meditation, prayer, deep breathing, and other exercises and dietary controls, and within a period of four weeks she had relief from her afflictions. It took her six months, however, to fully institute a regime that overcame her past negative programming and find an effective way for her to be rid of her affliction.

Mind Cosmology Regime for Health, Youth
and Long Life

1. There is a cosmic law of replenishment and restoration in the universe which works for your good. This is the cosmic power that flows throughout the universe. This cosmic power works at night; while you sleep, your body is being restored. However, you may harness this power during the day also by living a life in which there is moderation and balance in everything you do. Do not overeat, overdrink or overwork. If you smoke, try to do so in moderation. If you can stop smoking it is better for your health, and with these laws of Mind Cosmology many of our lecture members were able to stop smoking immediately.

2. To release the Alpha waves and other brain waves of healing, go into meditation each day for at least half an hour and let the higher mind within you send out the healing currents which give your body health, youth and vitality.

For meditation use the following mental affirmation. Think or say these words to yourself as you meditate, releasing the cosmic force that can give you healing, if you should be sick, or keep you healthy, if you are well.

"I now meditate on the healing currents that are within my mind and body and in the cosmic mind that rules the universe. I relax my mind and body and let the healing rays bathe every atom and cell of my brain and body with their healing currents. I now overcome all negative emotions of fear, worry, hate, jealousy, greed and selfishness, and replace them with the positive emotions of happiness, confidence, peace, forgiveness, charity, goodness and love. I breathe deeply of the golden elixir of life, knowing that the healing power of magnetism and other invisible forces now flow into my bloodstream, giving me perfect health, youth and vitality."

3. When you arise every morning, affirm the following mind cosmology positive thoughts, putting your mind and body into the cosmic rhythm of health and energy each day.

> I am life. I am health. I am youthful and have energy. I am magnetically alive and radiant. I shall function all day at a peak of cosmic energy and vitality. I now adopt the mental posture of radiant good health, youth and vitality.

4. When people ask you how you feel, do not go into a recital of your aches and pains, for you make them more real. You lower the healing currents of your brain and body when you dwell on thoughts of sickness, pain, accident, old age and death. These are the opposite polarity of life and health. Always reply, "I feel wonderful," or say, "I never felt better in my life." As you put yourself into this positive polarity of good health, you raise the brain wave lengths which regulate your body's health to a high level of energy, and actually you become healthier. Your body cells are miniature brains and reflect your mind's thoughts.

5. Break the past mental programming of negative thoughts that you have built into your consciousness about your body and your health. You do this by affirming the opposite polarity of thought from the negative.

Do not accept the fact that you can only live to be about

seventy years of age. Science now knows we should live to be at least two hundred years of age.

Do not accept the fact that you should have heart trouble because so many people have it. Science now tells us the heart is the strongest muscle of the body and should survive to two hundred years or more at this stage of our evolution.

Do not believe that after forty your body functions less efficiently. If the correct mental and physical habits are set into motion in your life your body should function perfectly the rest of your life.

Do not accept the belief that heredity accounts for your various ailments. Science now knows that heredity does not determine the type of illness you shall have. Disease is not inheritable!

Break the negative programming that you must have operations for gall bladder or other ailments. Your body has the ability to heal such negative conditions, if you should become sick.

6. To begin to break past negative programming give yourself a positive mental programming of the following mind cosmology suggestions, as you sit in quiet meditation. Hold your mind still and think or say the following positive programming:

> I now imprint my mind and body cells with the positive picture of radiant good health.
> I have no belief in the limitations set by mass mind on my life or health. I can and will live to be one hundred years or more in perfect health.
> I recognize the fact my heart is strong and will continue to beat in the life current of the cosmos for over one hundred years. I now direct life-giving oxygen and life force to my heart and it is pumping the magnetism and electricity which gives me life, to every cell of my brain and body.
> I instruct my subconscious mind to keep my body functioning at maximum efficiency at all times. While I sleep, my subconscious mind is instructed to repair my body, heal it, and keep my bodily functions operating perfectly.

7. Sit in meditation for at least fifteen minutes a day and let

the Alpha rays of your brain flow through your body giving it renewed life and energy. Hold in mind the thought of peace and tranquility. Visualize a still lake, reflecting the moon and stars in the heavens. Then feel that your mind is like that lake, without a ripple on its surface. As you hold this serene thought you will feel all your life forces flowing steadily through your body, and you will experience a sensation as if you are floating. Hold this level of high inspiration for a few moments, and as you do so breathe in and out deeply, holding the breath to a count of four, before releasing it.

8. As you sit in meditation and hold the above impressions in the forefront of consciousness, say to yourself the following statement: "I am serene and poised. My body is now in the center of a positive field of gravity in which all my life forces work harmoniously with the cosmic rhythm of the universe. I am peaceful. I am poised. I am strong. I am healthy. I am good. I am in tune with the dynamic life force of the cosmos and am perfect."

9. Invoke the law of cosmic action now in your mind and body. Mind Cosmology teaches that there must be mental and physical action to keep you healthy. Start each day with ten or fifteen deep breaths when you awaken. As you lie in bed tighten or tense the muscles of your entire body, starting with the head and neck, going down to the shoulders, the waist, hips, legs and feet. As you breathe in to a count of four, tighten the body, in what we call magnetic tensing, then hold the breath for four counts, as you hold the body tight, then release the breath, and at the same time completely relax your body. This helps flush out all the fatigue acids and refreshes your muscles and tissues with the fresh supply of oxygen, electricity and magnetism that is in the air you inhale.

A young man in my lecture group in New York believed that he had chronic indigestion because his father had it all his life. He began to suffer heart burn, gas pains and other symptoms that he had heard his father describe since the boy was old enough to remember. When he studied Mind Cosmology and realized that there was no reality to hereditary disease, he began to give himself the positive program discussed here and in two months time he was completely healed of his belief in chronic indigestion!

A woman of forty-five suffered from pains each month that were so severe that she had to go to bed for two or three days. When she came into our work, she told me that she had this type of ailment for many years, and she added with a long-suffering expression, "Oh, I suppose it's my cross to bear. My mother had the same condition all her life." When I showed her that she could not inherit an ailment from her mother, and gave her the Mind Cosmology regime to program herself out of this negative condition, she began to show immediate improvement. Her entire mental attitude changed and when I saw her again two months later, she told me she had no more negative symptoms from her condition.

How One Man Conditioned Himself
into a Heart Attack

One man I knew was only fifty-five years of age. He began to develop pains in his left arm, and had a heavy feeling in his chest and other symptoms. One day he had a severe attack and had to be taken to the hospital and the doctors reported him in critical condition. His frantic wife sought me out and asked for help. I told her to ease her mind first, and pray that her husband would recover so he could begin a new health regime using the principles of Mind Cosmology.

Her husband did overcome the temporary attack but the doctors warned him he would undoubtedly have another, and that he must stop work and take it easy.

When this man came to see me the first time, he walked like an old man. He told me he felt he was finished with life and he felt he was going to die. Then he wound up by telling me his father and grandfather before him had both died of heart trouble!

I gave him a Mind Cosmology regime that included deep breathing and exercising of a mild nature; and the mind conditioners which he was to use every day. I also told him that he could not give up life so easily; he had a fine wife, two sons in college, he was an executive in a manufacturing plant in New Jersey and he owned a beautiful home. I told him, "Why you should just now begin to live. You have so much to live for!"

Then I gave him mental heart-conditioners, which he was to use every day with his positive affirmations. I told him to sit quietly and send his mind to his heart, by thinking of his heart. I then told him to make a fist and visualize it as his heart; he was to open and close his fist as he thought of his heart contracting and expanding, sending the life force flowing throughout his body. He was told to open and close his hand at the rate of seventy beats a minute, which was approximately the normal rate of the human heart beat. He was to do this for five minutes each time, for three or four times, until he had established the rhythmic beat of his heart at normal. Then he was to go about his work, obtaining plenty of rest, fresh air, and to follow the diet his doctor prescribed.

This man returned to see me just one month later, and I wish you could have seen the change in him! His face glowed with healthy color; he was like a young man of thirty, and he told me that he was no longer worried or fearful that he would die prematurely. That was five years ago, and this man wrote me just recently that he has never had a relapse and now, at sixty years of age, he is still doing a full days work, has been promoted to a bigger executive position and has made plans to go on a round-the-world trip with his wife as a kind of second honeymoon!

10. Build the health habit. The habits we build in our subconscious minds determine our habitual patterns of action. Begin to build the health habit by thinking you are going to be healthy; by instituting a daily regime of work, rest, relaxation, good diet, deep breathing and magnetic tensing. Use your positive mental conditioners every day and keep your mind in a healthy, positive state of consciousness all day.

SUMMARY OF CHAPTER SIX

1. Science is now using the age-old Yoga methods of the Far

East to overcome sickness and heal people in the laboratories.

2. The brain wave lengths which you can release for healing your body through Mind Cosmology meditation and positive affirmations.

3. How to overcome fear, worry and other negative emotions through the use of transcendental meditation.

4. How spiritual and faith healing work to bring the body to perfect health and achieve miracle powers for healing.

5. How a woman with a tumor was able to use these principles of Mind Cosmology to completely dissolve the tumor.

6. One woman with sinus and bronchial ailment was healed through this regime of Mind Cosmology.

7. The Mind Cosmology regime for achieving perfect health, youthful vitality and long life.

8. The breaking of past negative mental programming and how to use programming for health, youth and vitality.

9. Positive mental programming statements to use for going into meditation and to achieve healing and long life.

10. How to use the cosmic law of mental and physical action to stir creative activity in the brain and body cells for health.

11. How three lecture members used Mind Cosmology to program health when they were sick and not responding to medical treatment.

7

How to Program Miracle-Working Powers with the Mind Cosmology Thermostat

God has fashioned in the invisible domain a tremendous miracle working power that you may tap when you want to work miracles in your own life. This power can be used to enrich your mind, heal your body, attract and magnetize money and abundance, and to regulate the events of your life so they are always in perfect balance.

This miracle-working power is regulated by a cosmic thermostat, which flows throughout all nature. We see this cosmic thermostat at work in the soil in springtime, releasing the life force in the seed that can cause it to become a patch of corn, wheat, or watermelons.

We see this cosmic thermostat working in the summer, maturing the seed, causing it to develop into a crop, and utilizing the sunshine, air and water, to bring to perfection whatever was in that seed.

Then in the fall we see this same cosmic thermostat turning off the power of growth and maturity and telling the earth, "Now is the time of the harvest; reap the golden crops that were hidden within the innermost secret places of the seed."

How This Cosmic Thermostat Can Also Work
to Mature Your Dreams

Your dreams, your wishes and aspirations, are the mental seeds, which you are planting, and you may set the cosmic thermostat of your higher mind to receive the cosmic vibrations that can direct you to the fulfillment of your every desire.

Where was the cosmic power that causes the earth to bloom in the springtime, during the long, cold winter? It lay slumbering in the invisible interstices of the cosmos. When the cosmic mind gave the creative command, this cosmic thermostat opened the flowers and revealed all the colors of the rainbow. The trees were suddenly festooned with green leaves and flowers. The earth became fertile, and out of the dark womb of earth, there came wheat, corn, tomatoes, cucumbers, peaches, pears, apples and oranges.

The Mystical Cosmic Programming of Your Body's Genes

You too, being a part of nature, possess this amazing miracle-working power of the cosmic thermostat which was set for you by God's cosmic intelligence. There was programmed into your body's genes, by cosmic mind, the color of hair and eyes you were to have, your height, weight, when you would mature and stop growing. The nine months you spent in the mother's womb were all there, programmed in your soul, before you began this mystical journey throughout eternity, and the cosmic thermostat triggered the exact moment of your birth when your period of growth had been finished in the womb.

To have more faith in this miracle-working power of your own cosmic thermostat, just stop for a moment and consider how this cosmic mind makes a bone grow. This is a miracle that confounds science.

Cosmic mind has created little bone messengers, within the marrow of the baby's bones, whose sole duty is to put calcium at the ends of the joints. As the cosmic thermostat is set for those bones to grow longer in a certain period of time, these little messengers are busy stretching the bones of that child from the inside, placing just enough calcium deposits in the joints to assure the child's full growth. When this job is finished and the child has achieved its proper height, the little messengers, obeying the cosmic mind, die off and are carried off in the bloodstream! Truly, this is a creative miracle that no human being can duplicate in the laboratories!

How to Program Miracle Working Powers with the Mind Cosmology Thermostat

1. The cosmic thermostat must be set by your own conscious mind, and then it will be programmed into your subconscious mind, where your autonomic nervous system will carry out the instructions you give it. First, have faith in this cosmic miracle. Know that you possess the power to shape your destiny. You can set that cosmic thermostat to failure or success. You can ask it to bring you riches and abundance, and break the spell of poverty; you can direct it to bring love happiness, and overcome loneliness and frustration; you can ask it to guide you to your right work, to develop your hidden talents and potentialities, and this cosmic thermostat will begin to work for you exactly as it does in the realm of nature.

After a lecture I gave in Washington D.C., a woman wrote me that she used my cosmic thermostat method to program a new social life for her husband and herself. He was a beginning attorney and wanted to achieve success in his career, but they had not been able to break through the difficult barriers that important people place around themselves in that city. She began to work mentally, putting into her mental blueprint the programming of a contact with some important person in the government who would help her husband get a big position. She wrote down this desire; she spent at least an hour a day in concentrating on it mentally; she visualized it already occurring, she saw herself being hostess to important people; she visualized the White House and some post that her husband would be chosen for that would give them access to important people.

Within two weeks time her husband met a famous senator from his home state of Illinois. The senator triggered a whole series of events which eventually led to this lawyer being appointed to a very important advisory position in the government, where he actually worked with assistants to the President!

2. As the cosmic thermostat is set by the cosmic mind of God, begin each day with a prayer to the source of your life and power expressing your faith in that source of all creation. It can be short and direct, such as the following, or you may use the Lord's Prayer. "Father, this day I wish to have divine guidance in every move of my life. Guide me to follow cosmic promptings; lead me into paths of goodness, righteousness and divine love."

3. Then mentally set your cosmic thermostat for the day's activities. Write down on a sheet of paper the different things you wish to use your cosmic thermostat for. You will then set your mental thermostat with that particular quality or thing that you wish to achieve every day of your life. On this list there can be the following achievements you desire:

> Perfect health
> Love fulfillment
> Riches and abundance
> Your right work
> Friends and social activity
> Peace of mind and tranquility
> Creative power to achieve your goals
> Psychic guidance and powers of clairvoyance
> Intellectual growth
> Happiness and contentment
> Travel and new life experiences
> Spiritual treasures and soul progress

4. Each morning when you arise, look at your cosmic thermostat chart and mentally set your thermostat at any of the above elements that you wish to manifest in your life in that day's creative action.

For that day you may set your mental thermostat at the section dealing with perfect health, riches, peace of mind, and happiness.

5. When you have selected the elements you wish to set your mental thermostat on that day, affirm to yourself several times a day the following positive affirmations, which cause these thoughts to become programmed into your subconscious mind:

> I now set my cosmic thermostat on perfect health. I program into my higher psychic mind centers the desire to maintain a perfectly functioning body all during this day. I desire perfect healing of any negative condition within my body. I regulate my heartbeat now to approximately seventy beats a minute. My blood pressure will be normal; my vital organs will perform their functions perfectly; my digestion will be normal and all bodily organs are now directed to perform their perfect function.

When you have programmed health into your subconscious mind and have set that cosmic thermostat to perfect health, do the same with the second element on your list—love fulfillment:

> I now set my cosmic thermostat on the finding of perfect love. I know there is a true soul mate for me, and I program into my higher mind qualities of good, unselfishness, high morality, gentility and love. Under the law of magnetic attraction I know that I shall attract into my orbit the perfect mate.

Then give yourself mental programming for the third element on your list—Riches and abundance:

> During this day I am in conscious awareness that I shall attract riches and abundance. I program into my higher mind centers the sum of $1,000 (or you may make it $5,000 or $10,000 if you have faith that you are ready for the bigger sums). I wish to use this money to improve my life. (Mention here, if you choose larger sums, just what you want that money for)—I

desire a home of my own. I wish to take a trip to Europe. I
want to educate my children. I wish to give my family the
comfort and security for their future that they desire. I wish
to buy a new car.

Go through your entire list each day and program *only* those
elements that you wish to emphasize for that day's action. You
can program the entire list each day, or only a few items.

6. When you have used this cosmic thermostat programming
technique for a period of three months you will find that most
of your innermost desires are fully programmed into your
higher mind centers. They are now taken over by the vast
sympathetic nervous system and go into the autonomic cosmic
realm, where cosmic mind begins to magnetically attract to you
that which you have put into your consciousness.

An advertising man I once knew used this method of cosmic
programming with his thermostat and experienced miraculous
results. He programmed riches and abundance, creative gifts,
psychic guidance, and his right work. He worked every day for
one hour on projecting the affirmations and thought forms of
what he desired. At the end of three months he was elevated to
manager of his advertising firm, and won three multimillion
dollar contracts from a cosmetic firm, a big cigarette company
and a food concern.

A member of my lecture group in New York used the cosmic
thermostat to work on her career as a television performer. She
wanted to have financial security, own a home of her own, find
a true soul mate and have travel and new life experiences. She
wrote down these and other desires on her blueprint of destiny;
she set the cosmic thermostat every morning when she got up
and several times during the day gave herself the mental
affirmations. In one month's time this girl became an outstanding television performer, starring in a daily adventure series
of a typical American business girl. She also had three television
commercials that brought her more than fifty thousand dollars
in one year!

7. Set your cosmic thermostat for daily goals as well as for
big, overall future goals. Chart the day's activities by writing

them down and program them into your higher mind centers. Use such positive cosmic mind motivators as these, or make up your own.

> Today,
>
> I shall set my goal to sell my product to five or more customers.
>
> I set a goal today for writing three letters to new customers for future sales.
>
> I shall this day hold high ideals and positive thoughts.
>
> I program into my subconscious mind the habit of punctuality and keeping every appointment promptly.
>
> I desire for this day to slow down my cigarette smoking, until I am able to stop this destructive habit entirely.
>
> I program a better memory and today I shall strive to imprint on my memory names of customers, new friends and facts that will prove helpful in my business.
>
> I program this day that I shall meet people of high standards and in important positions and that we shall be of mutual benefit to each other.

8. Control of your mental and emotional forces can help you program higher cosmic power into your cosmic thermostat. Practice each day control of your thoughts; do not let them jump from one subject to another, but hold them steadily on one thing at a time.

Control your emotions and program that you will have peace of mind and overcome negative emotions of fear, worry, hate, jealousy and anger in your daily activities.

Inculcate the emotion of love in your cosmic thermostat, and determine that each day you will express this emotion in your relations with other people in your home and in your work.

Remember, the creative ideas you express in your daily thoughts and emotions become caught up in the fabric of your mind and body and release miracle-working powers in your daily life.

Victor Hugo said of creative ideas: "There is one thing stronger than all the armies in the world: and that is an idea whose time has come."

9. Build your cosmic self image in the way you want to look, to talk, to act and to be.

Each day pass through your higher mind centers a series of positive self-image thoughts that will be set into your cosmic thermostat for future action as follows:

> I am important. I think important thoughts. My work is important and I shall win recognition and riches. My personality is magnetic and compelling. (If for any reason these statements do not correspond to reality, work to change yourself to fit the positive, new self-image you are invoking in your cosmic thermostat.)
>
> My consciousness is rich not poor.
>
> I strive to become a superior person and overcome all inferiority and inadequacy that was programmed into me as a child.
>
> I project the new self-image of value, dignity, magnetism, charm and beauty in my personality.
>
> I adorn my consciousness with the image of love and my personality reflects love, kindness, gentility and peace.

A woman I once knew had built the wrong self-image over the years. She was domineering, bossy and nagging. She married and divorced two husbands and then came into my work, and asked me what was wrong with her.

After talking to her for a half hour I found out that she had been programmed as a child to believe that men were inferior to women, because her own father had been a dominating tyrant, and caused her mother much heartache. She emulated the pattern of her own mother, which was harsh, unsentimental, nagging and fretful. When her two husbands left her she began to realize something was wrong.

I gave this woman the cosmic programming by which she was to set her cosmic thermostat to love, peace, gentility and understanding.

This cosmic programming worked miracles for this woman. She attracted a retired garage owner who had lost his wife. He needed a mate who would be understanding and furnish him with a good home. Her programming was so successful that he did not even object when he found she had been married twice and divorced. They were married and found happiness together.

SUMMARY OF CHAPTER SEVEN

1. The miracle-working power that exists in the cosmos which you may tap to attract money, heal your body, magnetize friends and regulate the events of your life.

2. The cosmic thermostat which flows throughout nature and how it works to produce crops in spring, and the harvest in the fall. How to tap this miracle-working power in your own life.

3. The miracle-working cosmic programming of your body's genes, which program your body in nine months time and pre-set your destiny before you are born.

4. How to program these miracle-working powers of Mind Cosmology and set your own mental thermostat to what you desire.

5. How one woman programmed a big position in Washington D.C. and a new social life that brought important people into her life.

6. The many different elements you may program with your cosmic thermostat and manifest in your life.

7. The positive statements you may use to program different things into your higher mind centers.

8. How an advertising man used the cosmic thermostat to program riches and abundance, winning promotion and three multimillion dollar contracts for his advertising firm.

9. How a lecture member programmed fame and fortune as a television performer and soon had fifty thousand dollars from television commercials.

10. How to set your cosmic thermostat for daily goals you wish to achieve of health, riches, happiness and fulfillment.

11. Control your mental and emotional forces to program higher cosmic power into your cosmic thermostat.

12. How you can build the cosmic self image you wish to project to the world of importance, value, personality traits or other qualities you wish to reveal to the world.

13. How the wrong self-image destroyed two marriages for a woman and brought her defeat, until she changed her cosmic thermostat to a different self-image of kindness, love and gentility.

8

How to Achieve Benefits
of Astral Projection
and Psychic Vision
While You Sleep

The cosmic intelligence that rules the visible and invisible world never sleeps, never forgets, never neglects mankind and his manifold needs.

Even while you sleep, this cosmic mind power can be tapped and reveal its secrets to your questing mind and soul.

Through the science of Mind Cosmology, you may put your soul into astral flight every night while you sleep and know profound secrets of your past lives that you lived in other incarnations, and mysteries of the cosmos that are reserved only for those initiates in the invisible brotherhood of mystic knowledge.

This chapter points out the method for achieving astral projection while you sleep and shows you how you may have psychic and clairvoyant visions which you will remember. These visions very often point out dangers you can avoid, situations in your future life that will occur and other important information that you should know for your present action.

How Your Soul Can Travel Back into History

Your soul has the mystical property of being able to project itself back into the dim corridors of history and examine the akashic record of the past. Everything that has ever occurred in the past is written in magnetic and electrical wave lengths upon the invisible cosmic memory bank and is never lost. Just as a sensitive piece of magnetic tape can record on its surface sounds, music, voices, and photographs of people in action, which can be reversed and played back whenever one wishes, so too the cosmic memory bank records every event that ever occurred on its invisible spiritual protoplasm. When the cosmic mind wishes to create something it refers to this cosmic memory bank, where the entire genetic history of a baby or a flower, or an oak tree is recorded, very much as information is now filed on microfilm in our libraries.

You may train your mind and tell it what you want it to discover for you on its astral journeys into the past or the future. Have you not had dreams that you visited some foreign place, and when you awakened, it seemed so vivid and real that you almost felt as if you had been there?

A study of Mind Cosmology reveals that these dreams are often the soul's remembrance of other planes of consciousness, even other lives that one has lived. It must be remembered that three-quarters of the earth's three billion people believe in reincarnation, that the soul incarnates in many bodies and when it has learned its spiritual lessons it goes on to other planes of consciousness, even other planets. Science now estimates that there are billions upon billions of solar systems bigger than ours, and that there is a strong possibility that there are one hundred million worlds that are inhabited by life similar to ours.

Sometimes the soul has to return many times, if it builds demerits instead of merits in other lives through the violation of cosmic laws. These cosmic laws are given in our Ten Commandments, The Sermon on the Mount, and in other spiritual documents revealed by masters, prophets and mystics of ancient times.

When you use your true soul's experiences for good, and practice loving acts of consideration, kindness, charity, goodness, and helping others to the spiritual light, your soul wins merits, and is able to free itself from this mystical wheel of life and need not return to this physical body again over the centuries.

How You May Probe the Past Mysteries
on the Astral Plane

You may go out onto the astral planes at night and take soul journeys to explore the mysteries of other lives you have lived. You can train yourself to remember such astral flights into past dimensions of time, and recall them when you awaken.

An example of vivid astral recall was that of a lecture member in New York who could project her astral self to distant places. She projected her soul to ancient India. She saw the sacred river Ganges, she remembered a village where she had been born and raised. She knew of events that occurred there and they came frequently as vivid dreams at night. She had a knowledge of yoga and Hindu philosophy, she was aware of reincarnation, and although born in an orthodox American-German family, and brought up as a Lutheran, she never felt comfortable in this incarnation.

She decided to go to India to search out her true spiritual identity. She felt a sense of having been there before; the moment she landed from the plane in Calcutta, she felt she was home. She was guided by intuition to a little village near Calcutta, and she recognized it as the place of her dreams. She spoke to natives there, told them of her astral flights, and then discovered that many of them knew the identity of her great-great grandparents, and that they were aware, by some strange spiritual transference of thoughts, of her identity and the reason for her having returned in this reincarnation to India.

Your Future Destiny Is Within
the Blueprint of the Cosmos

Cosmic mind, which we call God, has placed within your own higher psychic mind centers the entire blueprint for your present and future destiny. You can probe this mystery through the psychic vision that you have been given, when you use this force. When you go out onto the astral planes at night, you can be given psychic and clairvoyant visions of your future life. You can know the events that are scheduled for you in the present; you can be aware of the tapestry of dreams that God has woven and which will become your destiny.

Many times these astral visions will be of the future, revealing a design that accurately predicts events that are to come for the fulfillment of your destiny.

An example of how this works was that of a man who had studied with me in New York City, and knew how to achieve this form of astral projection to the future. He had a desire to become wealthy, so he would have future security for his wife and four children. He had worked as a waiter in night clubs for years and had managed to save ten thousand dollars. When he went to sleep at night, he told his higher mind that he wished to have an astral projection of his future and wanted to be shown how he could multiply this money into a million dollars.

One night, as he slept, he had an astral projection that was clairvoyant. He saw palm trees, beautiful beaches and long lines of luxurious hotels at the water's edge. He knew, from pictures he had seen, that this was Miami Beach, Florida.

Then he saw his name spelled out in letters of gold, as a skywriter might write something in the sky. Then, just like pictures projected on a screen, he saw the front of a restaurant and the words in letters of gold, Steak House. He awakened after this, and felt that his soul was trying to reveal something to him that related to his future destiny, but he did not know what.

He told his wife of his psychic vision and they decided they would visit Miami Beach that winter and see if there was something there that they should discover relating to his astral projection. When he arrived in Miami Beach, he later told me, he felt he was living in some kind of mental playback of a movie he had previously viewed. There were the palm trees, the beaches, the multimillion dollar hotels and everywhere, rich people on vacation.

Two days later he and his wife were strolling down a main street when he suddenly saw the restaurant front he had seen in his astral projection! It was red and gold, but another man's name was on the front. He looked again and saw that it was closed, having gone out of business.

Following his psychic revelation this man borrowed money from his friends and relatives, and with the ten thousand dollars he had saved, he opened a magnificent steak house, featuring only the best cured meats, which he kept in a special refrigerator. People could walk in and pick the steaks they wanted, and have them served with a baked potato and tasty salad. In a short time his reputation spread throughout Miami Beach, and people stood in line for his fabulous steaks. Within a year he opened two other restaurants and now, some years later, he is worth well over a million dollars and is ready to retire!

You May Tap This Higher Power
Through Astral Vision

You can turn to this higher psychic and astral power when you take your astral journeys at night. It can help you overcome your problems. It can show you how to go into your own business; it can reveal how you can make a million dollars; it can show you the pattern of the events that will make up your future destiny.

One man who had this higher psychic power went into the Nevada desert and was led to a gold mine where he found five million dollars in gold.

Another man has this higher psychic and astral vision, and receives guidance to discover water where no one else can find it. He has, in his long career, discovered thousands of hidden wells and grown comfortably rich from the services he furnishes in this capacity. He has not yet found a dry hole!

How You Can Unfold Astral Projection and Psychic Vision While You Sleep

1. When you go to bed at night, prepare yourself for your astral journeys into the past or future dimensions of time and space. Tell your higher mind that you wish it to guide your soul to its mystical experiences while you sleep. Give your mind the following cosmic treatment for this experience:

> I now prepare myself for astral flight. I wish to travel into the dimensions of future time and space and also explore the mysteries of past history. I wish to receive information and knowledge as follows:
>
> > What should I do to make my fortune in life?
> > How can I solve my problems and be free of burdens and debts?
> > Where can I get money to buy the home I want?
> > How can I be guided to the finding of hidden treasures?
> > Whom should I marry and where will I find my soul mate?
> > Should I buy this house? Should I sell this property?
> > Can I trust this person?
> > I wish to be shown how to make five thousand dollars in extra income this year to help with my financial problem.
> > I would like to write great stories—compose music—paint pictures—invent machines—discover chemical formulas that can make a fortune for me.

How One Man Used This Form of Astral Projection to Become Successful

A man I once knew in our lecture work had this type of astral projection and it presented him with a complete cosmic blueprint of his future life work. He asked for guidance as to what career he should follow. He had an astral vision in which he saw himself travelling in Africa, hunting wild animals, but instead of a gun, he had a camera. He saw the title of his book, with his name on it, telling of his exploits in the jungles.

When he awakened he was confused and puzzled, for he had never been to Africa, in fact, he had never been outside the United States. But he had faith that somehow this clairvoyant vision was trying to project him into some new mystical experience that would make him his fortune.

The next night, when he went out again onto the astral plane, he had the same type of vision. He saw himself travelling in a jeep with two other men. He saw amazing jungle animals; he visited a tribe of pygmies and seemed to be photographing them. This amazed him because he knew nothing about photography then, and he did not have money enough to finance such a trip to Africa.

A few days later, he was reading the *New York Times,* and under business opportunities he saw an ad that told about a rich, retired man who was going to Africa on safari and wanted someone to travel with him. Instantly he called the number given in the ad and arranged for an interview. He arrived in that man's office, convinced that this was to be his big opportunity. He was accepted for the trip, and went out immediately to prepare himself. He bought a movie camera, learned how to operate it, and was ready for his great adventure, which had been predicted by his astral vision.

This man took that trip to Africa, armed only with a camera, and his notebook. He jotted down his impressions on safari, he photographed the wild animals he saw, and reported everything accurately in his diary to later be put on his film for showing in America.

This man returned to the United States, prepared his film, and wrote his manuscript, which he sold to a big publisher. He booked himself, through an agent, throughout the country, where he showed his colored pictures and made a great deal of money. However, his biggest fortune was to come later, for a publisher produced his book, it was bought by the studios and made into a big picture, which immediately made him his fortune.

2. When you project your soul for astral flight, do so consciously, by preparing yourself as you go to sleep. Breathe deeply ten or fifteen times. Then as you prepare to project your soul onto the astral planes, visualize your soul tied to your solar plexus, by a golden umbilical cord. See this soul as being able to be projected up and outside of your physical body. Close your eyes and begin the conscious process of exteriorization, by saying over and over, "I now project my soul up and outward into the mystic realms of time and space. I desire that it take me back into history to explore the past and bring back a complete remembrance of my astral flight."

3. Now continue to breathe slowly and deeply as consciousness still remains. Begin to feel that your soul is rising upwards, and projecting outwards, away from your body. At this stage you should have a feeling of extreme lightness, almost as if you have no body at all. Then you should experience a sensation like rising in an airplane. The head may be light and dizzy, but do not be alarmed, for when you once master this first stage you can achieve the exteriorization more readily.

As you now command the soul to project upwards and outwards, your body should feel lighter and lighter, until all sensation of body ceases to exist. You may now feel something pulling up and out, tugging at your solar plexus, and at first the soul rises horizontally, the same as your physical body lying on the bed, then at a certain point, it begins to become erect and rises vertically. You will suddenly reach the threshold of crossing over from the world of matter into the world of spirit. You may hear heavenly music, you may see brilliant colors like a rainbow, or flashing lights; you may see a panorama of historical sights and hear sounds of voices, music, battles—an entire decade may pass in quick review before your soul's vision. Then you will lose yourself in the other dimensions of the past. These may be other lives your soul has lived through in your past, or they may be clairvoyant visions of actual historical scenes that flash upon the screen of consciousness.

4. When you go into astral projection at night, your higher psychic mind centers can be utilized to bring you glorious new ideas for your future growth and evolvement. You can give problems to this higher mind and it will solve them on the astral plane. Edison solved many of his most difficult problems through this method of astral projection, and when he awakened, he wrote down what had been given to him and the world was enriched through his revelations.

You can give this higher mind problems to solve, ask it for guidance in business, for formulas, for inventions, stories, or creative gifts such as art, composing, writing or other talents.

How a College Student Used This Power to Make Good Grades

A college student I knew who was studying medicine had a very difficult time making good grades. He studied these laws of Mind Cosmology and learned how to reach the higher levels of soul-awareness while he slept. He decided to harness this power, so before he dropped off to sleep at night, he passed in review the things he wanted information about in his studies. He slept soundly at night, but he was consciously aware that his soul was gathering information that he required for his class work. When time came for his next examinations this young man passed them with the highest marks he had ever received. He knew the answers to the questions that were asked and had no difficulty in answering them correctly.

How One Woman Increased Her Business 50 Percent

A woman, whom I had trained in using this higher psychic power, owned a small beauty shop and business was not too good. She had tried in every way to increase her business but her conscious mind was programmed to think in small terms and she could never get any constructive ideas for big business.

One night she went into an astral journey on which she asked to be guided to someone or something that could improve her business. She had a clairvoyant vision telling of a beauty specialist from Hollywood who would work for her, telling her clients how they could improve their appearance. She awakened and wrote down her idea, then went back to sleep, never knowing where she would find a Hollywood specialist in the small city where she lived. However she kept the thought filed in her subconscious mind for possible future use.

Two weeks later a woman came to have her usual permanent and hair coloring. She seemed highly excited and told the woman who owned the beauty salon, "There's a hair stylist here from Hollywood, who worked with some of the biggest stars in the studios. I'd love to have a consultation with him!"

The owner of the beauty shop asked where she could contact this man. She got the information, finally met the man, had lunch with him and found that he intended to settle down in his home town permanently. She made him a proposition to come and work with her. The next week she took a big ad in the paper telling that a famous Hollywood cosmetic specialist would be available at her shop for free consultations on women's cosmetic problems. The next day her shop was packed with eager customers. The hair stylist did fifty diagnoses the first day. The operator had hired three extra beauticians to work for her. After the Hollywood specialist had given his diagnosis of the woman's beauty problems, he advised her what to have done to her face or hair. Each of these customers spent two of three times more money having this extra work done than she would normally have spent. In a short time this woman expanded her business, opening three more shops in nearby small cities, and the Hollywood specialist became her partner.

5. When you have had your astral journey into time and space, and have examined whatever period of history you desire, or have had your clairvoyant psychic visions of your future, you may want to return to your body and awaken, to remember or write down your astral visions.

Give your soul a command to interiorize into your body, by saying, "I wish to return to my body and be consciously aware of everything that has occurred on the astral." Then make an effort to return, and you will have a feeling of falling from a great height. As your soul enters your body again, you may awaken with a jolt that actually shakes your physical body.

SUMMARY OF CHAPTER EIGHT

1. How to tap the astral planes at night while you sleep, by sending the soul to explore the mysteries of time and space.

2. The cosmic basis for the soul's astral flights, and how it works out its destiny in various lives through reincarnations.

3. How one woman projected her astral self to a past life in which she had lived in India and later went to the very village she had remembered in her astral flight.

4. You may discover the cosmic blueprint of your destiny through astral projection by reading the akashic record which your soul has created over the centuries.

5. How one man achieved wealth and success through an astral vision that came to him while he slept.

6. Step by step guidance to astral journeys while you sleep. The way to use this power to solve problems and answer your questions about your future.

7. How one man became a famous writer and explorer through astral visions that came to him while he slept.

8. How to exteriorize and interiorize the soul for successful astral projection and how to remember your astral journeys when you awaken.

9. How a college student used astral power to get good grades in his studies in medical school and achieve success.

10. A woman increased her business fifty percent because of guidance received psychically while she was on the astral planes.

11. How to consciously select the time when you wish your soul to return to your body from astral journeys while you sleep.

How to Take Twelve Giant
Steps to Attune Yourself
to Mind Cosmology Forces

There are powerful cosmic forces that exist in the universe, which you may attune yourself to and achieve the fulfillment of your every dream in life.

In this chapter we shall explore these cosmic forces, and learn how to take the twelve giant steps that can put you in attunement with the creative intelligence that can make you successful, healthy, happy and rich.

There is a cosmic rhythm that has been established in the universe that motivates all matter and causes everything to revolve in cycles that are orderly, harmonious and balanced.

How This Cosmic Intelligence Works

See how accurately this cosmic intelligence works in nature. In spring the sap flows from the roots of trees to their branches, preparing them for their new cycle of productivity. Flowers bloom at a certain time, leaves and fruit appear at predictable seasons, and autumn assures the harvest. This cosmic timetable of nature never varies, because it is set by a cosmic programming of events that are to occur in sequence.

You have been given the power to tap this higher cosmic intelligence in your own daily life and make it work to produce miracles of health, riches, love-fulfillment and abundance in your own life.

How One Man Used Higher Cosmic Power to Build a New Career

James S. worked as a service station attendant, but when he came into a study of the forces of Mind Cosmology, he learned that he could attract any destiny he wanted. He began to focus in his mind the cosmic intelligence through regular periods of meditation. He asked the question: What work would I be best suited to? The higher psychic mind told him to enroll in a course in electronics which he had seen advertised on television. He had never really thought about that type of work, but when he got the psychic impression so strongly, he followed instructions, and enrolled. After he had completed the course, he once again sat in meditation and asked how he could find work in his chosen field. He got no definite answer and went about his regular activities. One day he ran into a friend of his on the street who worked for a big television studio in New York. He told James S. there was an opening in his department. He immediately made application for the job and got it. Now he is working in an atmosphere that he enjoys and has a bright future ahead of him.

How to Take the Twelve Giant Steps to Attune Your Mind to This Miracle-Working Cosmic Power

First giant step: Have faith that there is a vast cosmic intelligence in the universe and that you can tap this higher mind power to work miracles for you.

All the great mystics and prophets have told mankind to have faith and believe that miracles are possible.

Now science tells us that faith and prayer often heal people of illnesses that doctors cannot cure.

Express this faith daily by going into meditation and asking cosmic mind for psychic and intuitive guidance in your life.

Express this faith by saying positive affirmations every day to charge your higher mind centers with new creative power as follows:

> I am now a channel for higher cosmic mind to work through me. I express my faith in this creative intelligence. I am now in a receptive mood to receive the divine guidance to help me solve my problems.

How Mrs. R. Was Able to Overcome an Unhappy Marriage

Mrs. R. came to me after she had been married ten years and told me her marriage was unbearable. Her husband had changed so that she could no longer tolerate him. Her love had turned to hate and she wanted to get out of the marriage. There were two children, five and eight, and this problem was not simple to solve.

I gave Mrs. R. a Mind Cosmology regime that consisted of rebuilding her romantic ideal with her husband once again. She was to meditate every day *not* on how her husband was, but how he had been during their courtship and honeymoon. She was to try to recapture the emotions and ideals she had had in those glowing days.

She was to thank God for her two beautiful children, and to see herself as a dedicated channel to serving them and also to making them good citizens for the glory of God and humanity.

As Mrs. R. withdrew the focus of her consciousness from herself and her limitations, to the outer periphery of creative action for her children, she began to develop a different attitude toward her problem. She asked for divine guidance in her prayers and soon she was able to live with her problem without feeling the sense of desperation that she formerly had.

Within a month's time she reported to me that her cosmic

strategy seemed to be working wonders with her marriage. Her husband, now that the pressure of her nagging and discontent had been removed, actually began to treat her differently. Under the impetus of her romantic remembrances she was more gentle, more loving, more tolerant and more forgiving. Soon her husband began doing all the little things that lovers do when they are trying to win the beloved and once again Mrs. R. found love fulfillment and happiness.

Second giant step: Find the inner core of stillness within your own soul and dwell there in silence for half an hour or so, whenever you have some big problem or wish psychic guidance.

To find this inner core of stillness within your soul, sit quietly in meditation and say to yourself this sentence, which is from the Bible: "Peace, be still, and know that I am God."

When you repeat this ten or fifteen times an amazing sense of stillness will come over your mind and body. It is in the creative stillness of your higher mind that cosmic mind can speak to you through divine intuition, revealing the knowledge that you wish.

When you are in a perfectly tranquil mood, repeat to yourself this positive statement: "I am now a chalice for the reception of mystical revelations from the cosmic mind that rules the universe. I ask for guidance to the solution of my problems."

A writer I know uses this type of meditation to increase his creativity. Before he sits down at his typewriter each day he goes into the silence and asks for guidance for his daily output of writing. The power never fails him and he is enormously successful now, whereas formerly, writing was laborious and he had few sales.

A businessman, who manufactures a household item in a factory located in New Jersey, was on the verge of failure when he came into our work and learned of this occult and cosmic power. He began regular sessions of daily practice, going into the stillness and posing the question to his psychic mind centers: What can I do today to increase my business output and thereby help people with my products? He reported that after only two sessions he received such valuable ideas that he immediately began new sales methods that have to date made him a millionaire!

Third Giant Step: Set your cosmic mind thermostat on the ideas that you wish to program into your higher consciousness.

When you get up each morning set that cosmic mind thermostat to success. Determine how many sales you shall make that day; how many letters you shall write; whom you shall see with business propositions; what steps you shall take to improve yourself or your product. We are all products of mental programming in this age of radio, newspapers and television. What you see, read and hear most often becomes programmed into your higher psychic centers and is released by the autonomic nervous system into actions—good or bad.

A young lady I knew in Hollywood had difficulty in making a living. She was timid and afraid of people. When she came into our work she sought me out for advice. She wore thick-lensed glasses that made her beautiful blue eyes look smaller than they were; she wore drab colors, her hair was caught back in a bun at the nape of her neck that made her look like a middle-aged school teacher.

After following our work for a period of two months this girl began to mentally program herself into a new person. She wanted to become a model but when she told her friends of this inner dream, they could not help but laugh, for she was tall, ungainly looking and with her thick glasses—well, she just did not seem photogenic.

I advised her to change her hair-do and affect a long, sweeping bob, with bangs that covered her high forehead. I told her to go to an optometrist and have contact lenses made, which would reveal her beautiful blue eyes, her finest feature. I advised her to go to a famous cosmetologist, who made up the movie stars, for a complete overhaul on make-up, which would bring out her high cheek bones, beautiful eyes and well-shaped mouth. Then I advised her to go to a good photographer and have photos taken, revealing her slender figure and interesting, aristocratic face. As a further step in her mental programming I told her each night to visualize herself in big magazines, and on television as a high priced model. Then with her photographs and contact lenses, and her startling new face and hair-do, I advised her to go to one of the finest model agencies on the West Coast and register for modeling.

She did as I advised and within three months she became one of our top fashion models and just last year, she made more than fifty thousand dollars on television commercials alone!

Fourth giant step: Unlock the new horizons of cosmic mind power through your powers of imagination and visualization.

Cosmic mind works through your imagination. It is in the imagination that all great progress must be imaged first. The Bible gives this law of creative imagery: "Let us make man in our image and in His image created He him; male and female created He them."

Every day pass imaginary scenes through your higher mind of the things you wish to do, or become.

Visualize yourself making ten or fifteen thousand dollars or more a year, and then imagine how you will spend that money.

Mentally take trips to foreign countries you want to visit.

Imagine yourself in your own business, selling something to the public, banking the money.

In your imagination see yourself living in the dream home you desire and project the visual images of your future family enjoying your home, entertain your friends there, see the garden in full bloom, and in other ways make that mental image real.

I saw a girl who was a waitress become a fine artist by projecting mental pictures of herself being able to paint. She paints as a hobby only, but she may develop into a commercial artist one day.

A young man who used this power of creative imagination was a shoe clerk, working in a store for a small salary. He began to imagine himself working in his own business—but what? He had no special talents, so he began to ask his higher mind for guidance. One day, in meditation, he had a flash of a sunlit beach, waving palm trees and beautiful Hawaiian music. He began to get travel literature about Hawaii, for he felt something was trying to lead him to those enchanted isles. Soon he was living in his imagination in Hawaii. He had saved a little money and decided he would take a trip there. Living in California, he was only four hours away from Hawaii. He took the trip and on the plane he began talking to a sunburned, athletic young man who, he found, lived in Hawaii. They got along well together, and later when he looked him up at his home, he discovered this athletic young man had a very big business in manufacturing and selling surfboards. He went to his home for dinner one night, and they worked out an arrangement where they could work together. Now, three years later, this young man has gone into partnership with the surfboard manufacturer and stands to make a fortune in the future.

Fifth giant step: Use the cosmic law of creative action.

The first law of the cosmos is action! Your higher mind centers must be inspired to begin their creative process by taking that first giant step of stirring your brain centers with action.

In your daily thoughts and conversation use dynamic creative expressions of action, such as: "I can achieve success. I am happy. I am healthy and young. I will make fifteen thousand dollars a year or more. I am able to paint, or write, or compose, or invent"—whatever creative talent you wish. Focus these creative ideas in your higher mind centers until they impel you in the direction of what you desire in life.

A man I knew, who had studied these laws in my work in California, had a piece of property that he could not sell. He changed his mental action from negative to positive. Each day he told his higher mind centers: I know I will sell this property. I see someone coming who needs this house and land and will pay me what it is worth.

He stopped all his defeatist negative mental action and changed the polarity of magnetism from negative to positive. Within three weeks time a man came to him and told him he wanted to buy his house and land, to build a factory on it for two hundred employees. He was paid what he wanted for his land.

Sixth giant step: Use the power of concentration on your life goal.

Concentrated cosmic mind power flows through your higher mind centers when you concentrate your mind on your goal in life.

In regular periods of meditation concentrate your mind power on the things you wish to do in life. Project mind power to the various situations you wish to change, such as finding new work, moving to another house or apartment, selling something you want to dispose of.

Seventh giant step: Use the law of cosmic alchemy to change the world of invisible matter and shape it as you desire.

The law of cosmic alchemy transforms and transmutes everything we see in nature, creating totally different products for man's use.

Luther Burbank used this law of cosmic alchemy to change fruits, vegetables and flowers into more perfect specimens.

There is an alchemical mental power which you can release to turn your thoughts into gold. All inventions come from this higher, mental alchemy. You can project your thoughts to the outer world, and release the power to create new products, invent objects, compose poetry or music, write, paint, design, or build an industrial empire through Mind Cosmology.

Psychic Communication Now Proved to Be a Fact

In one test taken during psychic projection, it was found that two people, three hundred miles apart, could communicate thoughts and thought forms to each other, as easily as though they were in the room next to each other. But the amazing thing about this experiment was that at the exact moment that psychic communication had been established, both the sender's and the receiver's heartbeats were as one! Previous to this psychic contact their heartbeats had varied but some mysterious thing occurred when their minds contacted each other and their hearts beat as one. It was also found that their brainwave patterns became identical! This is the astounding proof that there is something which the human mind can project in time and space and profoundly alter conditions in life.

A woman member of our Hollywood lecture group tried using this power of cosmic alchemy to locate her daughter and grandchild. The daughter had separated from her husband and took the grandson and disappeared. This woman sat in meditation and projected her thought forms to her daughter, telling her over and over, "Call me. I am frantic and worried about you and Billy. All is forgiven. Please call or write me at once."

Within two weeks the telephone rang and it was the woman's daughter! She said, "Something kept compelling me to think of you. Your face came to me several times and I saw worry and distress so I decided to call you."

A businessman I once knew tried using this power of cosmic alchemy to change his business. He was in wholesale distribution of household wares, and his business suffered a great loss and he feared he would have to go bankrupt. When he learned of Mind Cosmology power to influence conditions in his life, he began daily periods of practice meditation in which he sent the message to each of his salesmen—"You will sell more than your quota today. You have a good product; be proud of it and impress your customers' mind with the idea that they must buy our product."

He then visualized orders flowing into his office in large numbers; he mentally prepared himself for a big season and sure enough, within a few days time his salesmen were selling more than they had in many months! He generated a psychic energy whirlpool of mental power that reached out and touched the minds of his salesmen and customers.

Eighth giant step: Refuse to entertain negative thoughts about yourself, your business, your finances or your life. Do not let yourself be discouraged by seeming reality.

Think positively about your business affairs; do not succumb to the idea that we are headed for a recession or depression. Do not believe that it is impossible for anyone to become a millionaire because of taxes and bad times. The truth of the matter is that there have been over twenty thousand new millionaires in the past ten years—more than any time in previous history.

A young lady I know was brought up in a negative environment in her home. She heard nothing but cries of poverty and defeat in her early years. Her mother died at an early age, for no apparent reason; her father became heartbroken and died within two years after having lost the farm and the little money they had. When this girl came into our lecture work in New York she was a sorry spectacle of defeat, discouragement and general negativity.

She was so desperate that she had considered committing suicide, and had come to the twelfth floor of Carnegie Hall, where I had my studios for the many years I lectured in that world famous institution. She saw the sign announcing our metaphysical work and came into the studio to seek my help.

After hearing her story, during which she broke down and cried, I began an instant reversal of the entire life programming she had been subjected to, and started her on the positive regime of Mind Cosmology. She was to give herself positive suggestions at least half an hour a day, such as: "I now break the past negative cycles of fear, worry, lack and limitation. I program my subconscious mind with the new positive ideas that I want to carry out. I see myself as a new person, with the self-image of happiness, not defeat and misery. I project my ideal soul mate and a happy marriage. I shall keep my mind from dwelling on the past and project to the future. I have a new desire to live, to succeed, to love, to create, to achieve a great destiny."

This young woman was also told to enroll in an evening school to study something she enjoyed doing, so as to have something to occupy her mind besides work and drudgery. She got a job as a waitress, so she could make good money until she projected some other line of work. She studied music in the evening, for she had always wanted to play the piano. She had no great musical talent, but it gave her something positive to work on. She worked on her schedule for two months and then one day a doctor walked into the restaurant where she worked, and was impressed by her smiling, happy disposition. He needed a hostess in his large, successful office, as his girl was leaving to be married. She instantly accepted this offer and began her new job with a feeling that at last she was getting our of her rut and was on the way to achieving her life goal. She will eventually attract her love happiness and the other elements she has programmed into her subconscious mind.

Ninth giant step: Build the Mind Cosmology forces within your own mind of harmony, order, peace, beauty and goodness.

Just as order and harmony work in the atoms to create matter and visible substance, so too they work in your mind and body to keep you healthy, happy and prosperous. When you have discord and friction in your environment, soon you will be affected and your body cells will become sick and fail to function normally.

Change your mental atmosphere; be calm and peaceful in your approach to life. Do not let your reactive mind affect you; the world has always had wars and problems and you will not change things by letting your mind be sucked down into the maelstrom of confusion and discord. You can only help by being strong and resilient.

A woman I once knew lived in a cloud of confusion and discord. Everywhere she went she carried this vortex of negativity. She complained to waitresses, she found fault with sales clerks; she nagged her husband and children. Her husband finally left her for another woman, and when her children were old enough, they deserted her. She told me at her first interview, "Why has everyone deserted me? I've worked like a slave for my husband and three children and look at the gratitude I get!"

It took a great deal of mental housecleaning to get this woman back onto the spiritual beam of order, harmony, peace, and good. She was so far gone that she suffered from vague physical symptoms that the doctors could not understand. She had allergies, bronchial disturbances, sinus pain, and painful joint swellings which kept her from working.

When I pointed out our laws of Mind Cosmology, that she

was making herself sick because of her negative actions, she became violently agitated and berated me for my ruthless analysis. When she calmed down a little, I finally convinced her that everything she had done in her life had been negative and destructive. She had driven her husband and children away by her unbridled temper and criticism.

I gave her a streamlined course, as given in this book, so she could get results quickly. She programmed her subconscious mind to rid her of the symptoms of sickness in her body and especially her crippled joints, which the doctors diagnosed as arthritis.

It took three months of hard work for this woman to change her mental programming to one of health, happiness, peace and prosperity. But the change was astounding. She soon won back her husband and the affection and loyalty of her three children; she began to overcome her physical symptoms and now shows signs of being completely restored to her former health.

Tenth giant step: Use the power of your subconscious mind to give you guidance and direction in your life.

The subconscious causes the heart to beat, makes the blood circulate; digests the food you eat; regulates the glands; heals and repairs the body if it has an accident or becomes sick; kills germs that invade the bloodstream, operates the memory, imagination and gives us the five senses of touch, sight, feel, taste, and smell. It also gives us psychic vision and divine intuition.

Talk to your subconscious mind every night before going to sleep. You can use the second person "You," or the first person singular "I," in addressing the subconscious. Here are some positive autosuggestions you may use and you can make up your own to fit your various needs:

> You will heal my body perfectly while I sleep. I desire perfect health. Regulate my body functions so they will be perfect.
> I desire gifts and talents; you will release higher mind power which can guide me to unfolding my own inner gifts.
> I desire more money and supply; you will instruct my

higher mind centers with what work I should do, and how I
can attract the sum of ten thousand dollars which I need.

I wish love happiness and fulfillment of all my dreams and
ambitions; show me how this can be achieved.

Then, when you have given these autosuggestions to your
subconscious mind at least ten times each, believe that they will
come to pass. Also, write them down and make them a reality.
Your subconscious mind is imprinted by what you tell yourself,
by what you see, by what you read, and by what you hear from
others and believe.

Eleventh giant step: Turn to your higher psychic forces to
help you when your conscious mind does not know what to do.

You have been given psychic powers to help guide you to
your right destiny. You cannot hear this guiding voice within
unless you occasionally go into the silence and seek its aid. You
do this by going into meditation and stilling your conscious
mind. Then when you are perfectly still you will listen to that
intuitive mind that tells you what you should do.

I know a very famous politician in Washington who has been
elected senator from his home state for many years. He invokes
this principle of the divine will. He recently told me, whenever
he feels doubt about how he should vote, he goes into a
moment of silence, sitting alone at his desk, and invokes the
divine will. "How should I vote in this matter, Father?" he asks.
Then, as he sits quietly, something stirs within his mind centers
and he knows the course of action he should take. He has been
enormously successful in his career because of this mental
attunement with the divine source of life.

Twelfth giant step: Build creative inspiration to carry you to
the highest goals in life.

Human aspiration should always be toward the highest,
noblest and best course of action. To achieve this high goal, it is
necessary that you raise your inspiration to the highest levels of
human thought and action.

The most inspiring forces in the annals of human history have
been those inspired by a desire to do good, and to help the
human race.

Each day tell yourself that you are living to achieve high goals so you may help the greatest number of people.

The persons who get the richest rewards in life, including monetary rewards, are those who give the greatest good to the largest number of people.

This is why inventors, writers, artists, composers, musicians, singers, actors, particularly comedians, often grow rich beyond their wildest dreams. They tap a stratum of creative power that they release through their productive efforts to the whole world.

Comedians, who are able to make millions laugh and forget their troubles receive higher salaries than prime ministers, presidents and kings. Bob Hope, Bing Crosby, Frank Sinatra, Lucille Ball, Jack Benny, Elvis Presley, Red Skelton, George Burns, and Milton Berle are estimated to have built fortunes of from fifty to a hundred million dollars. Why? Because they have entertained, amused, inspired and delighted people with their creative talents for many years. The world is quick to reward those who enrich others with their creative gifts.

SUMMARY OF CHAPTER NINE

1. The powerful cosmic forces that exist in the invisible universe and how you may attune your mind to them and become enriched.

2. How this cosmic intelligence works in nature, bringing the cycles of planting, growth and harvest to the earth for man's good.

3. How James E. used this cosmic mind power to go into the field of electronics when he was a service station attendant.

4. The invisible wave lengths of power that carry light, television and radio and which conduct cosmic mind wave lengths to your own mind centers.

5. How atomic energy was released through the splitting of the atom and how your mind has the same power to release hidden energy to change your life.

6. How Mrs. R. used this cosmic power to overcome an unhappy marriage and achieve fulfillment once again.

7. The importance of attuning your mind to cosmic mind by finding the inner stillness and achieving creative power.

8. How a writer used this power to increase his creativity.

9. A businessman achieved a fortune through using Mind Cosmology techniques to put himself in tune with cosmic mind and divine guidance.

10. How to turn on the cosmic mind thermostat of success, health, happiness and achievement that can make your life dreams come true.

11. How to harness the creative mind power through the imagination.

12. How a young man used the creative power of his imagination to go to Hawaii and enter a successful business manufacturing surfboards.

13. How to harness the power of the cosmic law of creative action that can stir the brain centers with creative activity to achieve any goal you set in life.

14. The law of cosmic alchemy that can turn your thoughts into the shimmering gold of life.

15. How one woman used cosmic mind power to locate her daughter and grandson, and caused them to contact her within a short time.

16. How to remove negative thoughts that cause sickness, poverty, lack and limitation and go into the opposite polarity of health, riches and abundance.

17. How to harness the Mind Cosmology forces of harmony, order, peace, beauty and goodness in your life and achieve amazing results.

18. How to use your subconscious mind power to achieve guidance and direction in your life.

19. How your higher psychic mind power may be tapped so you can have ESP, clairvoyance and precognition.

10

How to Ascend to Mystic Heights and Receive Guidance from the Immortal Masters

Through the science of Mind Cosmology you can tap the thought forms of masters who have lived on this earth plane.

These inspiring thought forms that have created all our art, music, literature, poetry, inventions and industrial discoveries, are still caught up in the envelope of time and space, which surrounds our earth like a cocoon, and when you know how to tap this magnetic stream of cosmic intelligence, you may become a genius, creating magnificent works that will make you famous, rich and sought after.

This chapter will show you how to ascend to these mystic realms of dreamers and creative geniuses and use their actual thought forms to weave your own magnificent tapestry of destiny.

Science has now proved that all vibrations, all forms of energy, live forever. They never die. The soul substance of the immortals is still in existence in the invisible universe. The astral thought forms of Mozart, Galileo, Michelangelo, Leonardo da Vinci, Shakespeare, Columbus or Lincoln, are still in existence. Being magnetic and electrical in nature, they vibrate on the cosmic planes as wave lengths, very much as our atmosphere is filled with sounds of music, invisible entities and other forms of vibration, which we cannot see with the physical eye. However, when we build a receiving set, such as a radio or television set, we can accurately tune in on these invisible forces and make them come to vibrant life on the screen.

You Can Tune in on Thought Forms of Masters

You possess higher psychic sensors within your own mind and soul with which you may tap the mental thought forms of masters who now exist on other planes of consciousness. The disembodied thought entities of such great masters and geniuses who lived on the earth plane, are still in existence in another dimension of time and space. You may ascend to mystic realms and break through the time barrier, and receive guidance and vital information from these immortal masters.

How a Song Writer Used This Mystic Power to Compose

A young composer whose works have already been performed by several leading symphony orchestras of America, was a former student of Mind Cosmology in New York. He had a dream of creating beautiful symphonies, but his age (he was only twenty-eight) and his experience, seemed to limit him.

When he learned that he could unleash tremendous power and tap the creative genius of minds like Beethoven, Mozart and Chopin, he began to go into the silence and asked for guidance from these and other great masters.

Later this young man told me of how his first great composition was formed. He had concentrated his creative mind power on the genius of Beethoven. He saturated his higher psychic mind centers with the music of that great genius, listening to all his most famous compositions. He studied the life of Beethoven until he felt he was in complete psychic attunement, emotionally, musically and spiritually with this great composer.

Then he projected the desire to create great music to his higher creative mind centers, and asked that he receive inspiration from the soul of Beethoven. He knew, from his study of Mind Cosmology, that this genius still existed and that he could be attuned to Beethoven's soul and receive from it the musical inspiration that he desired.

He told me later, that the first time he knew he had contacted the soul of Beethoven, was one night when he walked alone beside the seashore. To put it into the young composer's own words, as he told me of this mystical experience, "The night seemed suddenly to be caught up with magnificent sounds; the roaring of the waves blended with the sighing of the wind; the silvery rays of the moon cast a mystic design over the distant horizon, and upon the restless bosom of the sea, from its turbulence and elemental surface, there arose a triumphant form of music such as I had never heard before! I was entranced and vibrantly in tune with the creative spirit of the master who seemed to be in direct communication with my soul. I rushed home and sat up the rest of the night, fashioning a beautiful composition."

This young man told me that his composition was later performed by one of the country's biggest symphony orchestras.

The Nine Mystic Steps That Can Help You Contact the Masters on Other Astral Plans

1. Each day, before going into mystical meditation, make out a work sheet for that day, on which you list the various things you wish to accomplish for that day and which you wish the masters to help you achieve. This helps solidify them in your higher psychic mind centers and forms the magnetic attraction which you need to attract into your spiritual aura the right thought forces for that day.

2. Go into a quiet room where you will not be disturbed

while you invoke the aid of higher thought forms of the immortals. Seek out the aid of the immortals that you wish to help you. Name them, and know that their thought forms are in existence in the astral realms, and can be tuned in on by your higher psychic mind centers.

3. Have quiet music playing in the background and a candle lit, also have incense burning or some fragrant scent, for these aid mystical meditation, open the higher nuero-psycho centers of your higher mind, making you receptive to the higher thought forms of the masters.

A famous author I once met told me that he was able to receive through this form of mystical meditation and elevation, the complete historical novel that was later made into a motion picture.

4. When you have stilled your conscious mind hold in your mind the pattern of creative thought you wish to receive. Is it a great invention? If it is, then ask for the astral thought forces of an Edison, Whitney, McCormick or Ford. You might frame your thoughts as follows, in asking aid from the disembodied thought forms of an Edison: "I now invoke the creative spirit of Thomas Edison. I ask for the guiding light of his great genius to direct my mind. I wish to receive an idea for a great invention that will benefit the world and bring me financial gain."

5. When you feel you have established this mystic contact with the cosmic mind that acts as an intermediary for all the great thoughts from geniuses to earth people, you simply sit silently, awaiting the stirring of your higher creative mind centers.

The thoughts may come to you in words, like a whisper, which you hear with your inner ear. You may receive visions as Joan of Arc did, in which you picture the actions that you will perform, like scenes on a motion picture screen. You may only feel an impulse, an inner urge, that suddenly brings into clear focus in your mind some inventive idea that you never thought of before. Sometimes, if you will take a piece of paper into meditation, you will get an urge to write down something that is coming through, in automatic writing.

*How One Man Used This Power to Receive an Invention
    from a Master*

A young man who studied these laws of Mind Cosmology with me in New York, sat in meditation and asked for guidance in an invention that he wanted to come through. He was mechanically inclined and worked in a big bottling plant for a leading soft drink manufacturer. He wanted an increase in salary, so he could buy a home for his wife and family of two children.

This young man went into the silence, and asked for the visitation of some higher mind that would give him an invention that could make him successful. An invention came through, a simple little mechanical gadget that would save time and money in the assembly line methods being used for bottling liquid. He immediately stopped and wrote down his idea. Then he went to the head of his department with the idea. The man was favorably impressed and told him he would contact the head of the company. Within three weeks, this inventive idea was approved by the head man and the young inventor got the sum of ten thousand dollars in full for his invention!

6. Each day invoke the aid of the mystic forces that exist in the invisible universe. When you start your day put yourself into magnetic attunement with the great minds of the ages, by saying the following positive magnetic affirmation:

> I now put myself into the center of divine creative action for greater creative good. This day I desire to be directed by some high inspirational creative spirit to do my best and to achieve my great goals in life. I call upon the highest astral forces in the invisible to assist me and to help me unlock the higher creative centers of my brain to achieve great things.

7. To better receive guidance from the immortal masters of past ages, daily put your mind in tune with the cosmic mind on the stream of time. Your higher mind is able to contact the great cosmic mind that tells everything how to mature and grow in nature.

This cosmic spirit that knows all things in nature is able to connect you with the minds of the past geniuses of any period of history. There is no time or space in the spiritual realm. Time flows continuously, like a great stream of invisible cosmic intelligence that flows on to the cosmic seas of eternity. You have the power to tap this flow of cosmic time and intelligence at any point in history that you choose and channel the knowledge from the vast cosmic memory bank of the universe, revealing the mysteries from the minds of those who lived in that particular period of history.

8. Practice the mystic arts of self-entrancement and necromancy, which is the ability to put yourself into a state of trance, such as that induced by self-hypnotism, in which you suspend your conscious mind and release your higher mind to the influence and control of invisible thought forces and entities.

To do this, prepare yourself at night as though you were going to sleep. Breathe deeply for ten or fifteen times and give yourself the hypnotic suggestion that brings on a state of trance:

> I now enter into a state of sleep, in which my higher mind will be free to contact the thought entities and disembodied astral entities of great geniuses who have lived before and who will now help me. I now sleep—sleep—sleep but my higher mind is conscious and aware of all the great thoughts that come through to me. I am now going into a state of entrancement where my mind will become the channel for great inspirational thoughts.

How a Woman Was Told of Hidden Treasure by Her Husband's Astral Thought Projection

A woman who had trained her higher mind in our class work lived in New Jersey. She had a small home on a plot of ground, where she lived after her husband died. After the insurance money was spent, she had no source of income and went to bed one night, projecting to her husband's astral self, that he come through and tell her what she should do.

This one night she had a clairvoyant vision of her husband.

He looked exactly the way he did when he was alive, and his voice was strong and clear as he told her that he had buried money in their back yard. He did not trust banks, having lost money during the bank crash of the early thirties.

When this woman awakened she could still hear her husband's voice in her ear. She believed what she had heard so strongly that she engaged a man with a bulldozer to come and dig up her entire backyard. After only two hours of work the bulldozer scraped up an old rusty box and inside it she found fifteen thousand dollars!

How One Young Man Found His Lost Sweetheart This Way

A twenty-three year old man had fallen in love with a girl that he wanted to marry, but he did not tell her of his love until it was too late. He had gone away on a business trip and when he returned to the city, the girl had disappeared.

This young man studied in our Los Angeles classes for some time, and learned about astral projection and clairvoyant dreams. He decided that he would use this method for locating his girl. Each night he projected her face and name and called to her mentally to reveal where she was living. He did this for one week and nothing happened, then one night he had a vision in which he saw himself in Las Vegas, and in one of the big casinos, he saw his girl friend working. He awakened and jotted down his impressions. They were so terribly real that he decided he would go to Las Vegas and look for the girl. He drove there in a few hours time, and went to several big casinos, without success. His girl was nowhere to be found. Then the next day he went into one of the casinos he had not covered, way out on the strip, and decided he would go in and have lunch. When he sat down at the table, he had an odd feeling that he was close to finding his girl. As he studied the menu, he felt a presence beside him; he looked up and there was his girl! She had taken a job as a waitress in that casino, just as he had felt in his astral dream. This time he made sure the girl did not get away again; they went to one of the numerous little wedding chapels that are in Las Vegas and got married the very next day!

9. Practice the mystical art of establishing oneness with the invisible forces of the universe. You can do this by taking on the qualities or conditions of the thing you are trying to become like or that you wish to attract.

Let us say that you wish to become more cultured and refined. You want to mingle with rich and successful people who live in fine homes and are accomplishing big things. To do this without adequate mental preparation would be impossible.

Take on qualities of culture and refinement by studying and perfecting yourself. Refine your personality by practicing good manners, work on your diction and speech, dress in the best clothes you can afford. Fill your mind with cultural ideas about music, art, good literature; be conversant with politics and world affairs. Practice before a mirror until you reflect the charm, poise and culture that you wish to reveal to the world.

If you wish to establish the vibration of money in your aura, take on the mental atmosphere of success and riches. Feel rich, see yourself doing the things that rich people do. Eat in the best restaurants you can afford. In your imagination take trips to foreign countries; get the travel literature from an agency, and plan future trips to distant lands.

SUMMARY OF CHAPTER TEN

1. How to use mind cosmology to tap the thought forms of masters and geniuses who have lived on the earth plane and be guided to achieving the great things they attained.

2. How the masters use cosmic wavelengths to communicate with the earth planes and how you may attune your mind, as one tunes in his radio or television set, to receive these higher vibrations.

3. How a song writer uses this mystic power to compose his great works that have been presented by a famous symphony orchestra.

4. How to take the nine mystical steps that can help you contact the masters on other planes through mystical meditation.

5. How you may become a great writer, or inventor, or creator

of great works through contacting the thought forms of the masters.

6. How one man received an idea for an invention from one of the investors who existed as a thought form on the astral planes, and made ten thousand dollars.

7. How to become magnetically attuned with the great minds of other ages by using positive magnetic affirmations to charge your higher psychic mind centers.

8. How the cosmic mind reveals secrets while you sleep and gives you the knowledge and power to achieve a great destiny.

9. How one woman discovered hidden treasures buried by her husband through an astral vision that brought her fifteen thousand dollars.

11

How to Achieve an Expanded
Cosmic Consciousness
for Daily Living

All cosmic secrets may be known to man, when he opens the mystical doors of the cosmos and achieves an expanded cosmic consciousness.

Mind Cosmology shows us the way to increase our mental powers and truly become superior beings.

Do you wish to know secrets of the universe?

Would you like to develop a keen memory? A greater intellect? A knowledge of how to build a financial empire?

All these things and more can be attained when you open the mystical doors of mind and spirit and come into an expanded cosmic consciousness.

Just as man has expanded the horizons of his knowledge and of the cosmos, through his daring flight to the moon and back, so too, the horizons of your own mind and your awareness can be expanded to include cosmic secrets of creation, the nature of

God, the spiritual entity we call the soul, and the power which motivates all forms of life.

It is this knowledge that I will impart to you in this chapter.

How You May Tap This Cosmic Mind Power
With Your Mortal Mind

You have been given the ability to tap this cosmic mind power with your own mind and channel it for your everyday needs.

This cosmic mind is everywhere present at all times, doing its mystical work of transformation under the universal law of evolution. The idea of perfection is behind all creation and all things in the cosmos are working towards an ultimate state of cosmic perfection.

The Inner Guiding Voice That Tries
to Show You the Way

There is an inner guiding voice that tries to show you the way to achieve your destiny. You can hear this psychic voice of guidance only when you have opened the mystical doors of your own higher consciousness and entered into that unlimited cosmic stratosphere of infinite mind, infinite power, and infinite riches.

Omniscience can be yours when you emulate the patterns of creative thought that you see reflected in all nature. See how beautifully the rose obeys the inner voice that tells it to bloom in the spring.

See how the birds build their nests, rear their young, and lovingly protect them, under the impetus of a higher omniscient mind.

Look at the delicate beauty of an orchid, which is brought to its ultimate perfection by some guiding cosmic power that gives it the blueprint of beauty that it instinctively follows.

Man also possesses this ability to tap this higher cosmic mind power, if he but expands his consciousness to include the miracle-working power of the infinite mind that created all things for his benefit.

How a Mother Built a Child's Destiny While He Was Still in Her Womb

A woman in my New York lecture group studied these laws of Mind Cosmology and she decided that her next child would become a concert pianist.

She had once studied music, with the thought of being a concert pianist, but had given up her promising career for marriage and motherhood. When she became pregnant she kept up her active interest in music; she attended concerts often. She listened each day to beautiful music on the radio. She read of the lives of great composers and musicians, and in her periods of daily meditation she visualized that her child, boy or girl, would become a famous concert pianist and win world-wide acclaim.

She kept up this process of cosmic direction of musical talent for her unborn child, for the full nine months of pregnancy. When her son was born, she surrounded herself with music each day; she programmed his childish mind with beautiful music, and as the child sat in his bassinet, he listened with rapt attention to the music.

When he was four years of age, his mother began his fundamental training, even when everyone told her the child was too young. She gave him the simple tasks of knowing the various notes in the scale and the child responded with great interest. At the age of six this boy was playing simple songs and later, when he was put into formal training with a great pianist, the man marvelled at the child's "instinctive" knowledge of music. This young child developed into a very fine pianist and I was present when he gave his first concert at the age of eighteen at Carnegie Recital Hall. When he was twenty-one years of age, he was booked by a concert bureau to play in leading auditoriums throughout America!

The Mind Cosmology Regime to Achieve an Expanded Consciousness

1. Use the power of transcendental meditation to rise above

the limitations of earth into the cosmic realm where true mystical power resides. Each day sit at least half an hour and still your mind.

Sit in meditation and concentrate your mind on the highest and most beautiful forces of life. Ask for psychic guidance from your higher mind and wait for the intuitive voice to speak to you, telling you what to do, how to solve your problems and come into the destiny you desire.

A woman who was having problems with her husband and her in-laws decided she would no longer fight with them, but began to go into brief periods of meditation daily, in which she invoked the omniscient power of cosmic mind to tell her what to do. She started sending out love to her husband and his relatives; when they criticized her, she smiled and turned it away with a light, casual remark. The more they ganged up on her, the more she withdrew her sense perceptions from sensitivity or retaliating with a sharp remark, and finally after two weeks, she noted a big change in them. They looked at her curiously, sensing that she was invoking the spiritual power of meditation, which fortified her against their sarcastic barbs. When they no longer got a reaction out of her, they soon stopped their tactics, and she began to get along better with the entire family. Love and patience are omniscient qualities and when we express them instead of hatred and impatience, we are able to pour oil upon the troubled waters of life and achieve true inner peace.

2. Expand the horizons of your mind through vision. The golden doors of cosmic consciousness open when you look beyond the limited horizons of your everyday challenges and limitations. Many people are imprisoned by their jobs and cannot rise into the realms of inspiration because they dislike their work. If you must work in something you do not like, try to change your work, but if you cannot, then negatively adapt to it. Let your mind explore other realms of thought, where you will feel a sense of liberation from the drudgery of your work. This can be done through hobbies, or avocations, where you spend your free hours doing creative tasks you enjoy, such

as painting, writing, music, dancing, or acting with an amateur group in your community.

A man who was a policeman did this by forming a group of policemen into a singing and musical group. They appeared on television in their community and played at many benefits and concerts to raise money for needy people. Their lives were immeasurably enriched by this activity.

A woman who had a job as secretary to a judge joined a group of amateur performers and directed their plays. She filled many tiresome hours of inactivity with her new hobby and soon was happier than she had been for years.

3. Channel the cosmic quality of omiscience in your own higher mind centers. You possess a higher psychic mind that can guide you in every important step in your life.

A young student of Mind Cosmology told me he had taken a driver's test for a license in New York and failed three times. He was afraid to try again, until he learned to let his higher mind centers guide him. He concentrated on this higher power and completely overcame his fear and tension and got his driver's license immediately.

I was talking to a very successful young attorney at a dinner party in Beverly Hills, California one night, and he told me that he believes some higher mind guides him in his court cases. He has won every case he has ever tried because he said, "I just relax my conscious mind and let something higher, that knows all the answers, take over. I feel that this power, subconscious or superconscious, call it what you will, knows all things and can give me the right words to say in court." He instinctively turns to this omniscient mind of the cosmos to guide him and that is why at thirty-five, he is one of the most successful attorneys on the West Coast.

4. Practice using the cosmic mind quality of omnipotence in your daily life. Your own powers of conscious mind and physical body are limited. But when you believe that some higher power than your own mind exists you immediately put yourself into attunement with that omnipotent power of cosmic intelligence.

What you believe in becomes the law of your life. If you hypnotize your higher mind centers with the belief that you cannot succeed, you will inevitably fail.

A man who came into my lecture work in California had tried for years to succeed in his chosen field. He sold products to service stations and all the other salesmen in his firm made big sales and commissions, but this man kept negating his mental power by telling himself he was not a good salesman. He was ready to give up, when he came into a study of Mind Cosmology and began to tap this stratum of omnipotence. He kept telling himself he could succeed; that he was a good salesman, that people would buy his product. This man began immediately to sell better than he had done in many months, and is now one of the company's top salesmen.

I once saw an exhibition of hypnotism, in which an athlete who was able to lift a weight of four hundred pounds, was told that he could not lift a pencil from a table. No matter how hard he tried to lift that pencil, his hypnotized mind could not summon up the power to do so, until the hypnotist gave him the suggestion that he could.

We all hypnotize our higher minds with our beliefs; if they are negative we get negative results and we short-circuit the subconscious mind power. If they are positive beliefs then we stimulate these higher mind centers and can achieve that which we believe we can.

5. Each day attune your mind centers to the cosmic quality of omnipresence. Your higher mind centers may receive an influx of creative ideas from the cosmic mind. This infinite intelligence is everywhere in the cosmos; it is the magnetic wave length that ties you to the mind of your creator.

This God mind is readily available whenever you need its guidance and creative power. You can talk to God as easily as you talk to a friend. You do this through programmed prayer and meditation, by putting yourself into a mood of expectancy and faith, you elevate your consciousness to the level of power you need for solving your problems.

A woman I once knew had to make a very important

decision. Her husband had died and she had three small children, and could not go to work, but she needed money to bring up her family. She studied these cosmic laws with me in Carnegie Hall, and knew that the omnipresence of God was everywhere, and could be tapped in her moment of need. She had a brother living in Wyoming on a ranch, and he and his wife had often asked this woman to come and stay with them. They had three children also and felt it would be good to have the entire family together. This woman went into the stillness and asked for guidance. Within two days time she had her answer; something told her to sell her furnishings and go to Wyoming with her children and live on her brother's ranch. She did so, and within six months time, she met a widower on a big adjoining ranch; he fell in love with her and proposed marriage. He admired her ready made family and they were delighted to have a father. This couple married and she found fulfillment of all her dreams.

6. Expand your consciousness by developing the power of your imagination. When you begin to unlimit your mind and grow wings of the soul, through your imagination, you can soar to any heights you choose.

In your imagination each day see your life changing for the better. Invoke the imagination to create a new environment; for as you begin to make a reality of another home that you wish to live in you will gradually outgrow the old one and find the means to achieve your new home.

Start imagining yourself in new work, making more money, buying the clothes, the car, the household furnishings you desire; gradually you will attract the money you need to achieve these realities that you projected through your imagination.

How a Manufacturer of Children's Toys Used This Power

A manufacturer of children's toys was in dire need of help. The public's tastes in children's toys had changed and he was still operating in the same realm of past, outmoded fashion.

This man came to some of my lectures on Mind Cosmology; he learned these secrets for achieving an expanded consciousness, and unlocking the creative power of his imagination. He sat in periods of daily meditation asking his higher mind for new ideas for toys. Through his imagination he began passing new images and thought forms. He gave his designers the ideas that came through to him about little toy space ships and astronauts; toy submarines with little propelling motors; walking robots that could talk and gesture like real men. His designers turned out models and the toy stores from all over America began ordering hundreds of thousands of dollars worth of new toys. This man has made millions of dollars because he expanded the horizons of his mind.

SUMMARY OF CHAPTER ELEVEN

1. The method by which you may achieve an expanded consciousness through the cosmic qualities of omniscience, omnipotence and omnipresence.

2. How to hear the inner guiding voice of the spirit that can show you how to solve problems and tap a higher level of power.

3. A mother used this cosmic power to create a concert pianist of her son before he was born.

4. How to use the cosmic power of transcendental meditation to rise above the limitations of earth into a cosmic realm where the creative mystical power resides.

5. A woman was able to save her marriage and turn disunity and in-law trouble into a happy, harmonious pattern of living.

6. How vision can expand the horizons of your consciousness to bring you out of drudgery, inaction and boredom into a useful, active full life.

7. How two people used this power to find new dimensions of activity for their creative gifts and talents and thus enriched their lives and found happiness and fulfillment.

8. How the cosmic quality of omniscience can be channeled to your psychic centers and guide you to your right destiny.

9. The cosmic quality of omnipotence and how you can hypnotize the mind centers to believe you can do anything you want to do.

10. A man who used these principles for improving his sales-work, began making better sales than he had ever made before, because he hypnotized his mind centers into believing in his superior powers of salesmanship.

11. How you can attune your mind to the cosmic quality of omnipresence and use it to contact the cosmic mind and be guided to solving problems and releasing new creative mind power.

12. How a woman used this Mind Cosmology quality of omnipresence, and was guided to find a great destiny for herself and her three children.

13. The imagination as an aid to unlocking cosmic mind power, and how a manufacturer of children's toys used this secret to become a millionaire.

12

How to Use the Power of Psychokinesis to Motivate Matter and Shape Your Destiny

The power of psychokinesis deals with the phenomena of projecting a form of concentrated mental and spiritual energy to influence and motivate matter, affect people and shape the invisible atomic forces of the cosmos into the patterns you choose to create your destiny.

The word is derived from two Greek words, "psycho," pertaining to the mind or soul, and "kinesis," meaning action. Psychokinesis, in our study of Mind Cosmology, relates to the power of the human mind and soul to motivate matter, and shape the invisible cosmic protoplasm into whatever destiny we choose.

Science has recently studied the phenomena of certain people who are able to project a stream of mental and psychic energy and move physical objects. Experiments now prove that a magnetic field of force can be built around objects, and that the human mind may then motivate these physical objects.

Dr. Rhine, of Duke University, was a pioneer in this form of research and he discovered that some people have the power to motivate dice, causing certain numbers to come up several times in a row and to perform amazing maneuvers that defied the laws of chance.

One man playing dice at Las Vegas decided he would try to bring number eleven up on the dice several times in a row. Number eleven is only possible with one combination of numbers: six and five, and it is a chance of one in several thousand that they would come up several times in a row.

This man projected all his mental energy as he rolled the dice, that they would come up eleven. The first roll came up eleven. Then he tried again, and this time they came up eleven. The third roll was also successful, and as the man had let his dollar remain on the eleven, his little investment of one dollar brought him a small fortune, as the number eleven paid fifteen dollars to one!

However, when this man tried doing this again immediately, the dice did not respond as they had formerly.

Every person has the power to motivate physical and material objects through the power of psychokinesis. Sometimes this happens accidentally, when the person projects a radiant stream of dynamic mental energy by wanting something very much. This intense emotion of desire seems to create a magnetic force that actually seems able to bring about the condition desired.

Magnetic Rays Affect Growing Seed and Ripen Fruit

Other evidence that there is some invisible magnetic field which the human mind may motivate and use was shown by scientists recently. When two magnets were put on each side of a seed the seed accelerated its rate of growth at an amazing rate. Other similar seed, without the magnetic currents, sprouted at the usual slow rate.

Fruit that was exposed to magnets ripened three times faster than fruit that was not magnetized.

Now scientists have taken photographs with special devices which show that a strange magnetic substance radiates from the human body, and forms an aura around the physical body. This is the astral body that psychics often see, and which the mediums call ectoplasm. It is a form of energy that exists in the fourth dimensional realm and is an emanation of the soul of man. However, it can be directed and caused to project thought forms to others and motivate their actions.

How a Man in Prison Used This Power
to Win Release

A man who had been falsely accused and sentenced to ten years in prison, read one of my books, in which I told about how the mind and soul may project thought forms to other minds, influencing them to take action.

This man began to project this power of psychokinesis to the minds of the judge, the lawyers, the district attorney—anyone and everyone who had anything to do with his case.

He stirred tremendous creative action within his brain cells, not only because he had been innocent, but because he had a wife and three children who needed him. Every night when he went to bed he would stir the creative centers of his higher mind with the declaration: "I am innocent. You will now free me. I wish another trial in which I will be found innocent."

One day a man from a newspaper, who had covered the case, went to see this prisoner's wife. He told her, "I don't know why, but I keep seeing your husband's face before me at night when I sleep. I feel your husband is innocent. My newspaper will hire an attorney for you and try to win a new trial for your husband."

The new trial was granted and new evidence was presented that won this man his freedom! Later, the man who had really committed the crime was arrested and confessed.

How to Use the Power of Psychokinesis to Motivate Matter and Achieve Desired Results

1. Mentally activate the atomic energy that is within your brain and body cells by having an intense desire to achieve something you want.

Sit in meditation and visualize this mind energy flowing through your mind like a cyclone of creative activity.

You must mentally create such a cyclone of atomic action in your own brain cells by visualizing this cosmic power flowing through your own brain cells. See this cloud of energy contacting other minds; visualize the faces of the persons you are trying to reach; direct your mental energy to their brain centers by projecting this atomic cyclone from between your eyes and attaching it to the forehead of the person you are trying to reach.

2. When you have made mental contact with the person you wish to motivate, talk to that person, as if he were there in person. Tell him what you wish him to do. Explain to him the reasons for his actions and reason with him. He will sense your mental projection, and react accordingly.

A young man in my New York lecture group used this mental power of psychokinesis to project an intense desire to go into partnership with a man who hired him to work in his store. This young man did not have the money to buy his way into the partnership, but in his mental projections he told his employer why he would be valuable as a partner.

Within one month's time, this man was talking to his employer and suddenly, out of the blue he said, "You know something, Bob, I had a dream last night that you had gone into partnership with me and my business increased one hundred percent! You know what? I'm taking you in as a partner, and maybe this dream will come true!" The young man could not believe his ears, for this was the very argument that he had been projecting to this man! The partnership was formed, and just as had been prophesied in the older man's dream, his younger partner increased the business one hundred percent in their first year of joint operation!

3. Each night, just before going to sleep, direct this power of psychokinesis to specific things that you wish to motivate. It can work through other people or it can sometimes directly affect your environment or bring about a change in some condition of your life that you want to alter.

A teacher had been fired from her job at the university because someone who hated her accused her of subversive activities. This teacher told me of her problem and I advised her how to send out a stream of psychokinesis to the members of the school board, with the mental request that she be reinstated. Two weeks later she was notified that the school board would reconsider her case, and this teacher was later reinstated, with a full apology and retroactive pay.

4. You can release the power of psychokinesis to shape a new business or career.

You can motivate a person to give you money that you feel you deserve, or which is owed to you.

You can rid your environment of some person who may be dishonest or troublesome in business.

A man who had a business partner that he thought was cheating him projected every night that the man would dissolve the partnership and free him. One month later this man, owing to health reasons, sold out his share of the business to his partner at a reasonable figure!

To release this form of mental power stir the centers of your higher mind with the commands of what you wish to be done for you. Mystics and seers from the Far East have long taught that there is an invisible mental force, which we call cosmic mind, that acts as an intermediary between all human beings. Now science has proved that there is a magnetic field surrounding all bodies, and it is believed that this can be motivated and affected by other minds.

They found that two people miles apart can influence each other's heart beat and brain waves.

Twins that were thousands of miles apart had similar mental reactions and performed similar actions at the same time.

Mothers whose children have been in danger, have had feelings that something was wrong, which later were confirmed.

5. You can sit in regular periods of meditation and project thought forms to materialize money that you may need for some specific purpose.

You mentally project the thought form of what you want the money for. Is it a new car? A down payment on a house? A trip you wish to take to some foreign country? A business you want to open? You mentally form the mental matrix of the thing you want to do with the money; then you project the sum of money you think you will need. You write it down and project it to the objective realm. "I wish the sum of $1,000 or $10,000. I want to accomplish the following." Then state what you want to do with the money.

A woman needed one thousand dollars to help her mother get an operation that would make her well. She had no way of getting the cash, but she kept projecting the mental thought form: "I want the sum of one thousand dollars so I can pay the surgeon to operate on my mother." She did this for one week every night, just before going to sleep. One night she had a clairvoyant vision in which she saw the name of a famous hospital and she saw a surgeon's face, and he seemed to be doing open heart surgery on her mother. She awakened and jotted down the details of her dream.

The next morning she called this hospital and asked for a surgeon who did this type of operation. She was referred to a man who occasionally did charitable work at the hospital for people who could not afford to pay. She instantly contacted the surgeon and after her appointment with him, she was assured that he would operate on her mother for no charge. The operation was performed and her mother recovered perfectly!

This power of psychokinesis was what the Master Jesus used when he was able to multiply a few loaves and fishes into enough substance to feed thousands.

This was the power that the Master released in the human mind and body to heal the sick and raise the dead.

The cyclotron of your higher mind may take the atoms of thought and split them into infinite particles of spiritual energy and from these invisible building blocks, fashion any world that you choose.

6. You can use this form of mental energy to actually turn your thoughts into gold, or money, the equivalent of your mental thought forms. Sit in meditation and ask for some great idea that you can release to the world that will enrich you.

Many writers, artists, actors, singers, composers, inventors, scientists, business men and industrialists have tapped this stratum of invisible mental energy to project their innermost thoughts and turn them into vast fortunes.

7. You can use this power of psychokinesis to gain control of your nervous and muscular system and cause your body to become healed, if you should be sick.

This is done by directing the mental energy to whatever part of your body is sick or in pain. You mentally visualize this stream of healing energy stemming from your brain centers to your body and at the same time you say a positive healing affirmation.

Breathe deeply as you say the following healing statement:

> I now affirm that I am in the center of a whirlpool of cosmic energy. I now direct this energy to my brain, to my heart, to my stomach, to my liver, to my gall bladder. (Concentrate on the organ affected or you may treat each and every body organ, one at a time, to assure the flow of life-giving, healing energy to all parts of your body.) This cosmic power is now healing my body perfectly.

One woman in our lecture group had a liver complaint, and doctors had diagnosed it as a chronic, incurable condition in which the liver cells had deteriorated and would not function. This woman projected healing currents to the liver every night; she never lost faith that she would be healed. Within one month's time she reported feeling better and upon a check up at the hospital it was found that her liver was functioning perfectly!

SUMMARY OF CHAPTER TWELVE

1. The mysterious magnetic force that can be used to motivate matter, and create patterns of positive action in one's life.

2. How one man used this mental projection to win a large sum at dice in Las Vegas.

3. The scientific proof that magnets can be used to make seed grow faster and to ripen fruit quicker than by natural processes.

4. The human aura and how this electro-magnetic force about the body may be directed and projected in astral thought forms that affect other minds.

5. How a man falsely imprisoned, won a new trial and his freedom by projecting through the power of psychokinesis, the thought form that he was innocent and deserved a new trial.

6. How can you create a cyclone of atomic power which can influence other people to do your bidding.

7. How a young man used psychokinesis to win a partnership with his employer and increased the business one hundred percent.

8. How to work this mysterious power at night while you sleep, and how one teacher used this power to be reinstated in her job, after having been fired for alleged subversive activities.

9. How to use psychokinesis to shape a new business career, or to attract large sums of money for any purpose you wish.

10. A woman used psychokinesis to get a thousand dollar operation for her sick mother, without having to pay a cent for the specialist.

11. How to use psychokinesis to release creative ideas for songs, stories, inventions, business, that can make you famous and rich.

13

How to Channel Cosmic
Subconscious Motivators
to Accomplish What
You Desire

Man lives in a veritable sea of cosmic mind power, surrounded by mystical forces that he little understands and seldom uses.

These miracle-working forces, which exist in the realm of the higher cosmic mind, are transmitted to man through a method which we shall study in this chapter.

These higher mind forces are cosmic subconscious motivators and when you program them into your higher mind centers they give you miracle-working powers which can be used to accomplish great things in your life.

All animals, insects and birds operate under this automatic, instinctive mind which causes them to do what is right to preserve them and assure the perpetuity of the species.

Man also possesses this higher subconscious mind power. In

man it is called intuition, and when it is correctly motivated it can guide you unerringly to the right decisions, and show you how to live under subconscious motivation with less effort and strain, without going through the frustrating process of trial and error in a random fashion.

Your subconscious mind is the connecting link between your conscious mind and the cosmic mind, which we call God.

You can contact this higher mind any time you choose by simply going into the silence and giving yourself certain cosmic subconscious motivators which trigger automatic action and bring into focus amazing reserves of power, intelligence, and intuiton.

The Astounding Things Your Subconscious Mind Does

The subconscious mind performs the following astounding functions for you automatically:

1. It builds the child's brain and body in the mother's womb in nine month's time.

2. It repairs the body when you are sick or injured.

3. It kills invading germs that get into the blood stream.

4. It controls the body's metabolism, digests the food and distributes the elements your body needs through your bloodstream.

5. It circulates your blood and nourishes every cell of the brain and body with the proper elements.

6. It regulates your heart beat and blood pressure, and sets a biological thermostat that keeps your body temperature at about ninety-eight degrees, and the heart beating at approximately seventy beats a minute.

7. It controls your lungs, causing you to breath, night and day. Like a guardian angel this higher cosmic intelligence causes the bellows of your lungs to inhale and exhale the life-giving precious oxygen and other elements in the air you breathe.

8. It regulates your memory, imagination and five senses. It causes your brain to store billions of impressions received from your sense of touch, smell, taste, hearing, and sight, into neat

filing cabinets in your brain. When you wish to draw on any of these, you can do so instantly, thanks to your subconscious mind, which knows where everything is stored.

How You May Tap This Subconscious Power with the
Ten Cosmic Subconscious Motivators

1. Desire is the key that triggers the automatic responses of this higher subconscious mind, causing it to release its amazing powers for your good.

Have a desire for wisdom and knowledge to live a better life and to implement the life force within your brain and body.

It is found now that when a person has a desire to live, he can extend his life span by as much as ten to fifteen years.

A man was dying, and seemed to lack the will to fight for life. A doctor whispered to the unconscious man, "You must live; you have a ten-year-old son who needs you. You must live to educate your son and give him future security."

This motivator seemed to sink into the dying man's subconscious mind. He rallied, came out of the coma, asked for food and within two days was out of bed, doing his usual work. This man lived for fifteen more years, with a seemingly incurable condition; long enough to educate his son, and then he quietly died. This proves there are vast reserves within the subconscious mind if we have sufficiently strong motivation to live.

2. One of the most powerful cosmic subconscious motivators that great men and women have used throughout the centuries, is a desire to do good and serve humanity.

Build this desire within your subconscious mind. Have a desire to do good for your family. Then extend this desire to help your community, to better the world, to bring peace, and to help humanity find new standards by which to live.

I knew a woman in New York City who was rich, but chronically unhappy. She came into our lecture work after losing her husband, a successful judge. She had no interest in living, as her three children were grown up and married, with families of their own.

I told this woman to start looking for other people whom she might help. Soon she found a community group that was working with underprivileged people and she began going to homes where there were problems such as dope addiction, broken homes, sick children who needed attention. She spent four to five hours a day on these missions of mercy and later told me that her life had at last become meaningful and joyous, for the knowledge that she was helping unfortunate people gave her great inner contentment.

3. Have a desire to become successful and demonstrate riches and abundance in your life, so you may do good for the world.

One of the greatest cosmic subconscious motivators for achieving material abundance is the desire to make money so one may help others.

Implement your desire to make more money by having in mind someone you want to help. Have a desire to educate your children; to live in a better house; to drive a better car, wear finer clothes and enjoy a higher standard of living.

The cosmic mind responds to man's desire to elevate and improve himself, and gives greater subconscious power to those using this desire for enrichment.

A young man I knew, who had studied in our lecture work in New York, was a drifter and had no desire to succeed in life. He was twenty-four and had not married. I advised him to fall in love with some good girl and marry and start rearing a family.

He found a very fine girl, who was going to school evenings to improve herself, studying typing and shorthand. She induced him to study with her, and they went to school together. Soon he was so much in love with her that he asked her to marry him. Under the inspiration of love, he continued in his studies, until they were both able to obtain work in a large office together. From this they went on to a better job, getting bigger salaries, until the girl became pregnant and had to leave her work after five months. With the coming child, this young man now had a bigger incentive to succeed than ever before, and he left his office work to become a salesman. Under the drive he now had to succeed, he sold more of his company's products than the other salesmen, and within one year, he was made district manager and had ten salesmen working under him.

4. Create a desire within your conscious mind to develop a radiant, magnetic and charming personality that will attract friends and give you power to influence others for good.

This motivating desire works in your subconscious mind to release magnetism in your personality. People instantly sense when someone is magnetic.

Each day build this cosmic magnetism by filling your mind with interesting and magnetic thoughts. Take an interest in people; radiate generosity and kindness; show a friendly, loving· attitude and people will respond with friendliness and love.

Miss Frances B. in our Hollywood, California lecture group did not seem to be able to attract friends. She was shy and withdrawn. She had been brought up by parents who were negative and constantly told her to be wary of people, that they would harm her, cheat her, betray her. As a result she had been subconsciously programmed with unfriendly and unmagnetic thoughts.

I put her on a regime of positive subconscious programming. She was to repeat all day, as often as possible, these subconscious mind motivators: "I radiate friendliness and love. I program into my subconscious mind the thought people are essentially good. I now have trust and confidence in people. I show an interest in them and their welfare. I become a center of magnetic radiance and project harmony, friendship, peace and beauty to everyone I meet."

Frances B. soon noticed the difference in those she met. She noticed they responded with more friendliness. She began to read books that filled her mind with interesting and magnetic thoughts, and soon was a good conversationalist. She drew on cosmic mind power to cause her to become radiant and magnetic, and her life changed from one of drabness and loneliness into one of happiness and fulfillment.

5. One of the greatest cosmic subconscious motivators you can use is the desire to have vibrant good health and youth, so

you can keep your body functioning in perfect health through-out life.

Your subconscious mind rules your physical body. To reach into its depths, releasing health and energy, give your subconscious mind motivating auto-suggestions daily when you start out in the morning.

Tell yourself many times a day: Today I shall function perfectly all day. I release creative energy from my higher mind centers. I am young and vital. I call upon reserves in my body cells to give me a strong life urge. I desire health and energy so I may better help the world and achieve my life goals. I am life. I am health. I am youth.

A man I once met in San Antonio, Texas, was constantly fatigued and had no relish for his work, which was as head of a large industrial plant that manufactured farm equipment. He was forty-five years of age, but acted as through he were sixty. I found out why, after talking to him for a few moments—he had lost his incentive for living. He had enough money; his family was grown up and married; he and his wife were bored and felt they were only living to make money, with no other worthwhile rewards in life.

I gave this man a Mind Cosmology regime to stimulate his future interest in life. I told him to stop working, take a trip around the world with his wife on a second honeymoon. When he returned, he was to begin with a new purpose for living; to bring happiness and prosperity to the world through his product. He took my advice, and called me several months later. He said he now had a new perspective on life and he had decided to return to his work to share his good fortune with other people. The first thing he did was to take his employees in on a profit-sharing venture, which gave them benefits they had never had before. He said that the entire plant had changed in its atmosphere, and they were now like one big happy family, whereas before they were uncooperative and numerous strikes had occurred which created many problems.

6. One of the greatest subconscious cosmic motivators is the desire to love and to be loved. Most of the world's greatest

masterpieces in art, music, literature and scientific achievement were inspired by the divine emotion of love.

Behind every great man's life is the inspiration of some woman's love. When you attune your subconscious mind each day to this inspirational force of unselfish love, you release tremendous creative power for every act of life.

A man I once advised, had lost his wife through his careless and unloving actions. He took her for granted, never thanked her for the little things she did unselfishly every day. He began to nag and show unpleasantness towards her, until finally she became disgusted with his continued abusive treatment and left him, not letting him know where she was.

It was only when he lost his wife that this man realized how very much he loved her. Then he came to me and frantically begged me to help him. I told him he must first change himself and his attitude towards his wife, so that if she ever did return, he would not lose her again.

I told him to make out a long list of his wife's good points and her failings. Then he was to do the same thing with himself. He was to be honest with himself, and admit every fault he had. When he had finished his list he saw that he was impatient, critical, fault-finding, sarcastic, criticized his wife's family, neglected taking her out occasionally to a dance or movie, seldom gave her money to buy little things unless she asked him for it, and many other things that he now realized had killed her love for him.

This man vowed he would change if he ever had the chance to win back his wife's love. I told him each night when he went to bed, to spend ten minutes projecting his loving thoughts to his absent wife. I told him, "Her soul will be aware of your psychic projections. She will know if you have really changed and she will call you."

Within one week this man called me from his office and said excitedly, "Just as you said, Jean came back, after telephoning me. She sees how changed I am, and we're like two kids who've just fallen in love for the first time!"

7. To stir your subconscious mind into action, give it this

cosmic mind motivator: Have a desire to do something creative and inspiring, such as painting, writing, composing music, or something else that will give something of beauty to the world.

Go into the silence at night when you go to bed, just before you go to sleep, and tell this subconscious mind: "I desire creative gifts and talents. I want to paint, (or write, or compose poetry or music, any gift that you really desire). How shall I go about it?"

You will be guided by this higher mind to the finding of your right creative talent.

A carpenter I once knew, was bored with his work, but he had no other talent. He asked his subconscious mind to guide him into other creative talents. One day, when he finished some of his carpentry work, something told him to get paints and brushes, and attempt to decorate it with his own designs. Because he created furniture for children's nurseries and play-rooms, this was a real challenge. He began his decorating and had the most amazing kaleidoscope of beautiful colors and designs pass through his mind. When he painted these on his children's furnishings, they became vivid and beautiful fantasies that delighted his customers. From this attempt to become creative he went on to greater success in his own business.

You may not be able to give up your work and go into something more creative but you can use your spare time to do something artistic and creative.

One woman who worked in an insurance company, and who had never married searched within to find out what she might do that would be creative. She was very lonely and spent each night looking at television. She came into our work in meta-physics and learned that she must stir the creative centers of her brain with some activity other than work. She joined a dancing class and went three nights a week to this social activity. She not only enlarged her social horizons, but she was able to achieve a greater sense of purposefulness in her own life. Many people have made contacts with others at such social events that later led to love and marriage. This woman now has a new desire—to find someone who can love her. She is projecting the ideal marriage and will undoubtedly find the right man, for she is now motivating a higher subconscious mind power that will direct her to her right destiny.

8. Your higher subconscious centers are stirred into creative action when you program into them a desire to have inner peace and tranquility.

When you start each day, program into your subconscious mind this positive affirmation: All day I shall dwell in peace and tranquility. Nothing shall have the power to enter my magic circle of inner peace. I am the center of God's radiant circle of love and peace. All my problems are now dissolved by the golden light of cosmic truth.

When anything in the outer world disturbs this center of tranquility, retire mentally for a few seconds and say, "Peace, be still, and know that I am God."

9. Your higher subconscious mind centers are influenced by a desire to have intuitive and psychic guidance.

Most of the automatic functions of the body are under the control of some higher power than your conscious mind. Why not trust this same power with the outer circumstances of your life? You can go into daily meditation and ask for divine guidance and intuition on any problems that are bothering you. The answer will come while you sit in stillness.

You can write down various questions for which you wish answers and take them into the stillness and wait for psychic guidance. You can ask such questions as: Where can I get the money to pay my bills? How shall I find my right work? Should I move to this new house? How can I find my true soul mate?

The answers may not come through at one session in the silence, so go about your regular activities and you will be shown the way—sometimes in the most amazing and unexpected ways.

A man who used this system of contacting the higher psychic forces in the stillness, told me that he wanted to find out how he could improve his gas station business and make more money. He got an idea for giving a premium with every ten gallons of gas that soon doubled his business.

A man who lost every job he ever worked on did not know why, until he came into our work in Los Angeles, and learned to go into the psychic stillness for guidance. Then something told him that he was antagonizing his customers and irritating them by contradicting everything they said. He did not realize he had this fault, which had been programmed into his subconscious by a very negative mother. He changed his entire personality and soon got a good job and is doing well.

10. The higher subconscious mind centers are influenced by a desire to know God, to worship Him and live under His laws.

You can find these great cosmic and spiritual laws in the Ten Commandments, The Sermon on the Mount, and the Golden Rule. Live your life with the highest ideals and sense of moral values you can adhere to, and you will receive divine inspiration. Each morning start your day with a prayer, and each night, before going to sleep, thank God for that day's life and inspiration.

SUMMARY OF CHAPTER THIRTEEN

1. You are surrounded by a miracle-working cosmic power which you may tap by reaching the subconscious mind within your brain.

2. The evidence of this power in nature; how it causes all creatures to perform their life function perfectly under their instincts.

3. How divine intuition may be tapped through your own subconscious mind to guide you in every move in the future.

4. The amazing things that your subconscious mind does for your body, healing you, regulating your heart, bloodstream and metabolism perfectly.

5. How to use the cosmic subconscious motivators of desire to channel this higher cosmic mind to your own daily activities.

6. How a dying man was given fifteen more years of life by stirring his higher creative mind centers with the urge to live.

7. How to build the subconscious motivator to do good and obtain the inspiration and help to achieve a great destiny.

8. How one woman who was lonely decided to try motivating

her higher psychic centers by a desire to help others, and it changed her entire life.

9. The innate desire within you to be successful and become rich, and how this can motivate you to great deeds in your future.

10. How a young couple used this desire to motivate their minds with creative effort that caused them to achieve great success.

11. How you can tap magnetism to create a radiant personality and motivate your higher subconscious mind to build a strong, vital personality that wins and holds friends.

12. The cosmic subconscious desire for good health, youth, and long life and how it works to keep you in perpetual dynamic energy.

13. The subconscious motivating power of love and how it can release energy and vitality to motivate your entire life.

14

How to Have Cosmic Perception to Develop ESP and Clairvoyance

You have been given the ability to use the power of cosmic perception to know the future and to be aware of events that have occurred in the past in the lives of others.

You can use this cosmic power to develop extra-sensory perception, known as ESP, and to be clairvoyant. This power is in all living creatures and is called instinct in animals, insects and birds. In humans this power is called intuition.

The great cosmic mind which created all things, knows everything, including how the future is going to shape itself. To tap this amazing cosmic psychic power you must study the laws under which it works in your mind. This chapter is devoted to that subject.

Your thoughts can be projected to other minds and imprint them with the things you want them to do. This is called psychohypnosis. Have you ever bought something you did not want and when you got home you wondered how the salesman had managed to impose his will on your mind? He was using this power of psychohypnosis. You can project thought forms and they will go out in the universe, like ripples on a lake when a pebble is thrown into it. These thought forms will lodge in the minds of those who vibrate to, or are in tune with your thought projections.

How a Woman Broke Up a Marriage with This Power

This power, used for negative and destructive purposes, was vividly brought to my mind by a lecture member in New York City. Laura M. told me that a woman had been practicing witchcraft and voodoo rites to get her husband away from her. She found out when a friend told her she knew the practitioner of this form of black magic and she had confided the secret to her.

The spells and incantations which were given to the woman to use over Laura's husband's mind were forms of black magic, but they began to work, for this man gradually lost interest in his wife and finally left with the woman who had been projecting psychohypnotic thoughts.

When Laura M. told me this, I knew that she would have to use the forces of white magic to win back her husband's love. I told her to begin to project to his mind the thought: "I love you. You know I love you. For the sake of our two sons come back to our home. You will be forgiven and I shall always love you." This woman began to project this thought as many times a day as she could. She went to sleep at night projecting this loving thought. Within one week her husband called her early one morning and said, "For several nights now I have dreamed of you. Your face came to me clearly, asking me to come back. I must have been bewitched by this woman, for I don't love her, and want to come back to you. Will you take me back, Laura?"

Of course Laura did take him back. She never told him her secret, nor the fact that the other woman had indeed used mental projection, a negative branch of it, for her evil purposes.

Thoughts Travel on Invisible Wave Lengths

Thoughts travel on invisible wave lengths, very much like the wave lengths that carry sounds and sights to your radio or television set. You can aim or direct these invisible thought forms to any person you choose, no matter how far away they are. Working under the same laws governing wave lengths of light, these electrical vibrations from your mind may be sent to great distances and they will lodge in the person's mind that is emotionally attuned to you.

How a Woman Projected a Command to Her Son
One Thousand Miles Away

A woman I know had lost touch with her married son, because of a family quarrel. He and his wife and son had disappeared from their home in Southern California. The mother made frantic efforts to find them but did not know where to search. I told her that she could contact him with her thought forms, and showed her how to direct them to his higher psychic mind centers. She did this for a period of two weeks, and one day an airmail letter came from Seattle, Washington, telling her that her son realized he had made a mistake and wanted to make up with the family. He added at the end of his letter, "I don't know why, but I have had a restless urge to get in touch with you now for the past two weeks."

Cosmic Perception May Also Be Used to Receive Thoughts

Cosmic perception and psychic powers may also be used for receiving thought forms that are sent by other minds.

Clairvoyant vision, in which pictures of coming events may be accurately seen by your higher psychic centers, can be developed so it works while you sleep. "Coming events cast their shadows before" is a statement of this clairvoyant power to receive visions of events scheduled to occur in the future, and which are known to the cosmic mind man calls God.

How to Develop Cosmic Perception for ESP, Clairvoyance and Psychic Powers

1. When you wish to use this power of cosmic perception, go into the silence for a few moments and still your conscious mind. Say the mystic sentence that comes to us from Tibet, used to open the third eye, known to science as the pineal gland, where psychic powers are believed to exist. *"Ohm mane padme ohm."* This means the jewel in the heart of the lotus, the soul within man. Say this mystical invocation five or ten times until you feel stillness within.

2. Then hold in the forefront of your mind the face of the person you are trying to communicate with. See that person as you know him to be in life. Then talk to him, just as if he were there in person, aloud or silently. Say his name several times: "John, John, John, I am trying to reach you. I need you John. Get in touch with me at once. Your father is sick. We need you at home. Call or write me at once."

3. After you contact the person with your mind, use an emotional appeal to reach his higher mind centers. In scientific tests with ESP, it has been found that those who are emotionally tied, such as mothers and their children, husbands and wives, close friends or members of a family, are better able to receive and transmit psychic messages.

4. When you have repeated your message ten or fifteen times, go to sleep and do not strain to continue the contact. The thoughts, being already transmitted on electrical pulsations, will go out and somehow contact the mind of the person you have projected to.

5. To receive psychic guidance and clairvoyant visions for your future, go into the mystic silence as instructed above. Then ask your higher mind to give you specific information that you desire. Write down a list of the things you want to know about the future.

How can I get into a business of my own?
Where can I get the five thousand dollars I want?

How can I meet my true soul mate and marry?
Should I buy (or sell) this property?
Is it safe to take this airplane trip?
Can I trust this man in business?
Where is the ring I lost?
How can I receive a story (or song or invention or other creative gifts you desire) so that I can become rich?
How can I build a strong, dynamic and magnetic personality?
How can I solve my problems?

6. After you have written down your questions and taken them into the silence with you, read them quietly and mentally concentrate all the powers of your mind between your eyes, projecting a golden line out into the infinite. This golden line is the line of infinity and connects your third eye, which is the psychic organ of inner vision, with the mind of the cosmos, which man calls God. Send this golden line up into the cosmic spaces very much as a rocket shoots up and out of earth's gravity pull. This is your lifeline to God and, like an umbilical cord, ties you to the source of your life, intelligence and all good.

7. When you have released your requests or questions on which you wish advice and guidance, go about your ordinary activities. If you do not get an immediate answer in the silence, do not worry.

Sometimes the guidance or information will come to you later, when you are working or sitting quietly. Like a bolt out of the blue the thought will come, "Call Martin; he will help you find a job." Or, you may be given the answer through a letter or telephone call that comes in a day or two. Or someone you meet on the street will be the channel through which your mental request will be granted.

One lady I know uses this psychic gift whenever she has a baffling problem. She opens the Bible anywhere she is guided to, and the first place her eye rests on the page, generally holds the answer.

A businessman I know sits quietly at his desk, and asks for psychic guidance in every business decision he has to make. As he holds the stillness he asks, "Father, what is Thy will?" The answer generally comes through in a few seconds of quiet meditation.

I know an author who invokes this same psychic guidance every time he sits at his desk to write. He quietly asks, "Father, guide my mind and let it be a channel for the expression of your perfect creative thoughts." He generally begins to write automatically within five minutes and has made an enormous success since he began this method of psychic unfoldment of higher ideas.

8. Clairvoyant vision can come to you at night while you sleep. You will have an unusually vivid dream, sometimes in color, in which you will receive a flash of scenes just like on a movie screen. Sometimes these will be warnings; sometimes revelations of things that are going to happen to you. Sometimes they will be symbols. A dream of an airplane could mean a trip; also a boat, or automobile. A cross might mean a spiritually illuminating experience that you will have. To dream of losing money could be a warning to be cautious in investments.

9. Many times clairvoyant visions will come through while you are awake and sitting quietly in reverie. These may come as pictures projected onto a wall, or as flashes of mental scenes that project vividly on your brain.

One man had this type of clairvoyant vision in the daytime. He kept seeing flashes of some country where there were palm trees and jungle growth. He did not know why this happened, until one day he received a letter from a relative who had come to this country and settled in South America, in Brazil, where he had made a vast fortune through his business of importing and exporting. He wrote his cousin in New York asking him to come to Brazil and join him in his business venture. The man did so, and made a big success.

A Woman Had a Clairvoyant Vision of Accident to Her Son

A member of our New York lecture group had a clairvoyant vision several times that her son was involved in a serious traffic accident, but when she told her son he laughed at her "crazy psychic stuff," as he called her clairvoyant impressions. A few weeks later, while driving over a bridge in wet weather, his car skidded and crashed into another car, seriously injuring the other passengers. He escaped unharmed.

10. Get in the habit of asking for specific things from your psychic mind. When you go to bed at night, take a list of mental requests into the silence with you. Ask for guidance, for ideas to come through that can make you money, for information on how to get money or improve your business.

One Man Had a Dream of Winning at the Races
  the Sum of $1,000

A man in our Hollywood lecture group last year had a dream one night which he felt was psychic. He saw a horse that seemed to be five lengths ahead in the stretch. Over her head he saw a name, which he jotted down when he awakened. He went to the track that day and there was a horse with that name in the fifth race. It was given at the odds of ninety to one, a most unlikely winner! He bet fifteen dollars on her, and the horse won by five lengths in the stretch!

Another person I knew, who had studied these laws of psychic phenomena, had a dream in which he saw a big bell ringing. Because he worked in the stock market he thought the bell significant, so he looked to see what stock had the word "bell" in it. He found a stock called Packard Bell, which was selling for nine dollars a share. He bought a thousand shares and held it for a few weeks time. This stock went up to forty-two dollars a share and he sold it making a profit of over thirty thousand dollars!

11. Examine all your hunches, intuitions and psychic impressions carefully before you discard them. Your higher psychic mind centers are always in tune with the cosmic mind that

knows all things. This higher power may be trying to reach you to warn or guide you to some future course of action where you might be helped to achieve something great, or to avoid some danger.

There are psychic symbols which might come in dreams or which may occur while you are in reverie with your eyes open. A bird in flight could indicate inspiration, striving to achieve some high goal. It could also be a symbol of a trip you will take.

A psychic flash of fire could be a warning that a fire will break out in your home. A man I knew had a psychic warning of fire on several occasions. Three fires erupted in his apartment house within two months time. Fortunately, his possessions were not harmed, as they were fires in the apartments of others.

A symbol of a door could indicate entrance to a new life experience that will occur in the immediate future.

A stream of water often indicates the flow of higher creative mind power, but it could also indicate a trip over water.

SUMMARY OF CHAPTER FOURTEEN

1. How cosmic perception can give you power to know your future and have ESP, clairvoyance and psychic ability to send and receive thoughts to and from other minds.
2. How one woman used this power to project to her husband the thought that he would return, after breaking up their marriage.
3. How one woman found her lost son and his family by projecting thoughts to a distance of one thousand miles and reached her son's mind causing him to get in touch with her.
4. How to go into the silence and project any message you wish to another person, no matter how far away he may be.
5. The method for giving your higher psychic centers specific questions and problems that you want answers to, and how this works to bring you amazing guidance in all your affairs of life.
6. How to become a receiving station for information from other minds as well as from the cosmic mind that exists in space.

7. Three members of my lecture group who use this power daily to receive benefits in business, and for personal problems.

8. How clairvoyant visions can come through at night in the form of dreams, giving guidance, just like scenes on a movie screen.

9. How a man was guided psychically to go to South America, where he made a fortune in a business with his cousin.

10. A woman was warned of an accident to her son, which actually occurred, but could have been avoided if her son had listened to her.

11. How one man won $1,000 on a horse at Santa Anita, in California, when he was given her name in a psychic dream.

12. How one man dreamed of a bell ringing, bought a stock called Packard Bell, and made over thirty thousand dollars!

13. Hunches, intuitions and psychic impressions often come through symbols. How to read and interpret these symbols.

14. How symbols like fire, doors, water, and other like objects could reflect psychic projections from your higher psychic centers.

15

How to Channel the Secret Doctrine of Cosmology Power to Make Your Desires Come True

From the philosophy of the Far East there is revealed a secret doctrine which we use in Mind Cosmology to make our dreams come true.

This mystical doctrine tells us that behind all creative action there is a cosmic, or universal spirit. This creative intelligence, flowing through man's higher mind, guides and motivates his every move. When man aligns himself with this creative spirit, it enlivens the cells of creativity within the brain, causing all the hidden thoughts to be released, shaping and molding the inner dreams into outer forms of reality. This means that you can use this higher power of creative cosmic mind to make your dreams come true.

The Bible speaks of this mystical law: "As a man thinketh in

167

his heart, so is he." Your innermost secret thoughts and dreams furnish cosmic mind with the blueprint from which it will fashion your destiny.

The Bible also states the working of this law of creativity in these words: "Let us make man in our image; in His image and likeness created He him; male and female created He them."

This mental image of creativity relates to all forms of creation. If you want to invent something, it stems from this inner, subjective realm of your creative mind.

If you want to build a house, the mental picture must be there before it can be translated by the architect into the precise instructions for the workmen to follow to build that house.

Your Higher Creative Mind Can Fashion Any Destiny

Your higher creative mind has the ability to fashion any destiny that you desire. This power works under certain laws which we shall study in this chapter.

Cosmic imagery is the method by which God creates everything we see in the visible universe. Using building blocks of atoms and molecules this creator causes trees, fruits and vegetables to spring into existence, following the well-known law of the cosmos: "As ye sow, so shall ye reap." The cosmic spirit can only manifest what is in the creative principle or seed.

For the projection of your inner dreams to the outer world of reality, it is necessary that you plant the right seed within your creative mind centers.

There are three vital steps needed to bring this about:

1. Hold in your mind the dream or thought you want to project to the outer world and make a reality.
2. Concentrate all the creative powers of your mind on this subjective dream by sitting daily in meditation for at least a half hour and visualizing in all its details, the achievement of the goal you desire.
3. Then project this creative power into the objective

realm by taking steps to make your inner dream an outer reality.

For example, you may want to become a famous writer. This is the inner dream or thought you want to project. You sit quietly and meditate on this idea; you visualize yourself writing a great novel or scenario; you see the money pouring in from your idea; you enjoy the feeling of popularity and fame it brings you.

These steps stir the creative imagery into motion that can produce a great novel but until you sit down before that piece of paper and put your ideas on it there is no way for that dream within to make contact with the outer objective world of reality. The beginning of creation is in the idea, but the execution of the idea depends on your ability to project it into actual creative action by doing something to make that dream come true.

How a Student of Mine Used This Power to Make a Fortune

A thirty-five year old man who came into our studies in New York inherited the sum of twenty-five thousand dollars. He told me that he wanted to make a fortune in the stock market. I did not try to dissuade him by quoting statistics that ninety-five percent of all those who trade in the market usually lose money. He bought stocks without any knowledge of what he was doing, and waited for his money to double. The stocks went down and in panic he sold them and lost about ten thousand dollars. Now he was really worried and he sought me out again to ask advice. I told him that before investing in the market he should give his higher mind more accurate information and figures to work on. I advised him to study everything he could find on stock market investment and finances. He was to read the *Wall Street Journal* every day, and other publications and books that informed him on the inside workings of the market. He did this for three months, then took the remainder of his money and went back into the market.

This time he had taken step number three given above, for

projecting his inner subjective dream of making a fortune to the outer world of the objective. He took steps to learn facts about the financial world, and this final step gave him accurate knowledge which was programmed into his subconscious to make the right investments and soon he had won back the ten thousand dollars he had lost and was on his way to making a profit.

Step-by-Step Guide to Use of Cosmic Mind Power to Make Your Dreams Come True

1. Put into your higher mind centers the seed or dream that you wish to make real in the outer world of matter. No skyscraper is ever built without that idea first being in the mind of the architect who drew up the plans for the building. Your master architect, which is the cosmic mind of God, is waiting for your blueprint of destiny. He has the power to create that destiny, but you must first plant the mental seed or thought forms.

2. Do not be afraid to ask this cosmic mind for big things in your life. Dare to dream big and you will be inspired to create great things. Ask for money, set a certain sum that you want in a definite time, such as one thousand dollars within three months. If you are afraid to ask for bigger sums start with smaller sums first, such as one hundred dollars within one month. Then when you get this money set your goal a little higher, until you are able to demonstrate larger sums from this higher mind.

A young man of twenty-five came into my lecture work in California to seek knowledge for building his personal fortune. He had been earning a salary of one hundred dollars a week, which was not bad for one of his unskilled background. But he became infused with the idea of going into his own business, and used Mind Cosmology principles to do this.

He became inspired to study public speaking, so he could better express his ideas. At the end of six months he had changed amazingly and had tremendous magnetism and power. He had written down his blueprint of destiny, and set the sum of fifty thousand dollars a year as the income he desired. He had faith this would come to him within one year. He became so enthusiastic with his new idea that he decided he would travel and lecture before large organizations, giving their employees the regime he had used to expand his consciousness. He began to send out circulars to all the large business and industrial organizations in California, offering to train their salesmen and employees, to help them increase their efficiency, and raise their level of productivity.

Soon he had answers to his letters and interviews with the executives of these large organizations. He gave his first public demonstration before twelve hundred employees of a large industrial organization and received a large fee for his services. From this beginning the young man went on throughout the country, doing the work he had projected in his blueprint of destiny. Now his income is well over the fifty thousand dollar a year figure he set for himself when he began.

3. Write down on a sheet of paper the different things you want to demonstrate from cosmic mind. Enumerate them, and write them down in detail. If it is a new car you desire, do not just say car, but specify Cadillac, Ford or Chevrolet; color, style and model.

If you desire a home of your own, describe it in detail. Put down the numbers of rooms, location of bedrooms, kitchen and bathrooms. Then cut out pictures from home magazines and paste them in your scrapbook of destiny, which will picture the things you want to demonstrate from cosmic mind.

4. Make up a treasure chest in which you put a small piece of gold, silver, simulated diamonds, rubies, emeralds and other precious stones. These should be looked at often, imagining them to be real jewels, to magnetize the centers of your consciousness with the idea of riches.

5. Also put into that treasure chest a deed for property, houses, apartment buildings. Write your name on these pieces of paper, making your claim on certain properties which you would like to own in the future.

Also put into your treasure chest pieces of paper which you visualize as stock certificates. Write on them one thousand shares of General Motors, one thousand shares of Bethlehem Steel, one thousand shares of General Electric, or other stocks that you select.

Whenever you want to strengthen your belief in your future state of riches, go through this treasure chest and project the things you put into it in the future reality of the objective world. You can also have a bundle of paper, the size and shape of money, and in the four corners of which you write one thousand dollars. You can have ten or twenty of these; count them frequently, and visualize them being turned into the real substance. Visualize your bank account filled with this cash, and see the things you will do with that money.

6. To build your faith in the cosmic power that can make you rich, carry in your pocketbook at all times a check made out to yourself for one million dollars. Sign it, *God, the Universal Banker.* Every time you see this you will affirm to yourself that God has literally given you a universe and all that is in it; it belongs to you as much as anyone else, and therefore you already are worth more than a million dollars.

7. Each day run through your imagination the various steps you will take to fulfill the desires and dreams you have put down on your blueprint of destiny.

If it is a trip to Europe, mentally take that trip. Choose the plane or boat you will go on. Get travel literature picturing the interesting cities you will visit. Go to the library and look up the countries you will visit; get to know the customs, the history and other interesting features of the country you will visit.

How a Woman Projected a Trip to the Middle East

A woman in our New York lecture group, who worked as secretary in an insurance company, projected that she would take a trip to the Bible lands of the Middle East. She had no knowledge of where the money was to come from, but she planted the mental seed, wrote it down, prepared her mind with knowledge about the countries she would visit, and then she confidently awaited results.

That next summer, her family, who lived in Minneapolis, sold a piece of property they owned, which had been difficult to sell, and sent her portion of the inheritance, which was five thousand dollars! She suddenly found herelf on the boat cruising in the Mediterranean, visiting Israel, Egypt, Turkey and Greece—on the exact trip that she had mentally projected in her blueprint!

8. Each day project these mental images that you have put into your higher psychic centers to the outer world. Like a motion picture projector and screen, see your mental images being projected to the world of reality. Live in the dream house; see the automobile and ride in it mentally; take the trip to the places you want to go. As you project these mental thought forms they take on a life and dimension of their own and begin to lodge in the cosmic mind, which has the power to manifest them to the world of reality, and project them on the screen of the outer world.

How an Attorney Won Public Office Through This Method

I once knew a young attorney who had never held public office. He had this desire so strongly that he made up his mind to win a political office in the next election in Los Angeles. This young man had taken only one course with me and learned about how to use Mind Cosmology laws to project his inner dreams.

He began to project the thought that he would win that public office he had chosen. He visualized it strongly. He visited the building where his office would be. He saw his name on a plate on the door of his private office. He projected his name to the millions of voters mentally, and began to feel and act as if he were already elected.

That year, when election time came around, this young man was given his party's endorsement for a public office. His name went on the ballot and he won over his opponent by a large majority. His mind and soul had made such a reality of this victory that he could never imagine himself losing.

9. When you run these cosmic thought forms through your consciousness it is vitally important that you do not, at the same time, run negative thoughts that short-circuit your mental power, and negate your positive forces. If you think each day of the possibilities of failure and visualize yourself losing business or money, you actually build the negative polarity of magnetism which is repulsion, and it neutralizes your positive mental forces and sets the automatic mechanism of your sympathetic nervous system in the direction of the loss and failure.

*How a Man Used the Negative Polarity of Mind
     and Had Tragedy*

One man who came to my attention some years ago, was in a pitiful state from the results of years of negative mental programming. He had been brought up in a negative home environment as a child, where he heard of nothing but sickness, poverty and misery. Later, when he married and had a good job, he reflected the negative patterns he had learned as a child. His father had been an alcoholic. This young man now began to drink when he had problems to face. He worked in a bank, but soon lost his job as he became careless and made many mistakes caused by drinking.

He became worse and worse, and finally his wife and child left him. He became a chronic alcoholic and would often wind up sleeping in doorways or in missions in the Bowery.

One day this man walked by Carnegie Hall and saw my poster announcing a lecture: "How to Be Born Again Through Cosmic Power." He came to the lecture and I used as my theme the Bible saying, "Unless a man is reborn in the spirit, he cannot enter the Kingdom of God."

Later this man sought me out for advice. "Do you really believe this power of God can help me be born again?" he asked.

I told him, "It is never too late for anyone. You must change your self-image and have an intense desire to change your life.

You must literally be born again mentally, psychically and spiritually."

I gave this man our Mind Cosmology regime for projecting his new-found dream to the outer world and he began to work on it.

I sent this man to an agency which helps rehabilitate people, and they got him a job as a bank guard. He soon bought new clothes, lived in a clean room, became well nourished once more, and looked as he had before he had changed so radically. This man eventually went back to his home town; he looked up his wife and reconciled with her and their son. Now, with the love and help of his wife and family, this man will never revert to his former, negative habits of thinking and living.

Remember this vital law of Mind Cosmology: We externalize in our outer lives that which we program into consciousness.

A woman I once knew had an abnormal fear that she would be robbed and possibly assaulted by a burglar. She lived in this aura of fear and insecurity for years. One night she forgot to lock her bedroom window and when she awakened she sensed someone was in the room. She was so paralyzed with fear that she could not even scream out. She lay there in mortal terror while the burglar ransacked her room, and only after he left was she able to jump up and scream. Her fear not only attracted this disaster but if she had been insulated against fear, she would have been able to let out a good healthy scream, which would normally rout any thief.

SUMMARY OF CHAPTER FIFTEEN

1. The secret doctrine from the Far East that reveals how you may tap the creative intelligence that can guide and motivate you to the achievement of all your dreams.
2. How you may use cosmic imagery to fashion the destiny you desire, using the building blocks of atoms and molecules to create a glorious destiny.
3. The three vital steps in Mind Cosmology that can help you project your inner dreams to the outer world and make them a reality.

4. How a man used these principles to make a fortune in the stock market, after first having lost ten thousand dollars.

5. How to plant the mental seed that can build the destiny you desire, utilizing the principles of Mind Cosmology to form your blueprint of destiny.

6. How a former student of mine left a job making only one hundred dollars a week and built a salary of over fifty thousand dollars a year.

7. The secret of how to build your treasure chest and scrapbook of destiny in which you will put the priceless treasures you want to materialize in your outer life.

8. How to build a big money consciousness by carrying a check made out to yourself for one million dollars.

9. How one woman attracted the sum of five thousand dollars, after projecting a trip to the Middle East to visit the mystic lands, and was able to go on an extended tour of five countries.

10. How an attorney won public office by studying and using principles of Mind Cosmology and projecting the inner dream to the cosmic mind, which made it a reality.

11. How negative polarity can negate your good and bring sickness, poverty and suffering in your life.

12. How one man used the laws of Mind Cosmology to overcome alcoholism and build a completely new life.

16

How to Achieve Instant
Demonstrations of
What You Want
Through Cosmology

The art of demonstration is the mental process by which you can bring into existence that which exists only as a mental thought form at first.

You can invoke cosmic mind power to achieve instant demonstrations of the things you want in your life. This begins with the consciousness that the fulfillment of the wish exists at the moment of conception of the thought.

The child is in the process of being born from the moment that conception takes place. The inherent cosmic blue print for that baby is there, in the invisible cosmos and it materializes under the laws of involution and evolution, forming a perfect child in nine months' time.

This Power Works Under Cosmic Laws

You can invoke this cosmic power to demonstrate what you want in your life.

Do you want to earn more money in your work?
Do you desire going into your own business?
Are you trying to find love-fulfillment in marriage?
Do you want to demonstrate your own home?
Do you want health, peace of mind, happiness?

These elements may be brought into existence by using the cosmic laws that rule the invisible universe.

In this chapter you will be shown, step by step, how to invoke the dynamic cosmic laws that can bring you instant demonstration of what you want in life.

A Young Man Wanted His Own Business But Had No Money

I met a young man in New York, through my lecture work there in Carnegie Hall. He told me he was a pianist, but worked in a health food store part-time to support his wife and two children, since there was no money in music.

I paid this young man to play piano at our various public functions. Gradually he began to listen to the lectures, learning the secrets of Mind Cosmology. After I had given a lesson on how one can achieve instant demonstration of the things one wants, he came to me, his face glowing with a new expression of self-confidence and hope.

He said, "I have always loved music, but never believed there was any money to be made in it. Most musicians I know can hardly make enough to keep them going. But now I believe I can somehow make my music pay." Fired with this new determination, this young man got an idea for a popular song, which he named, "Till the End of Time." He wrote down the notes and words as they came through and later it was published, making him a fortune! But it was not the success of that song that proved to be the big thing in his life; a Hollywood studio put him under contract to write music for them, paying him well over one thousand dollars a week.

How to Use the Laws of Mind Cosmology for
Instant Demonstrations

1. Use the Law of Activated Desire.

Action is the first cosmic law. The stirring of the atoms and molecules that formed the cosmos and all the billions of stars in our galaxy, was started with a creative command: "Let there be light." This command from the creative center of the universe, which we call God, started the creative process through the law of activated desire.

Start the flow of cosmic creative power in your brain cells by giving this command to your higher mind. Express your desires in concrete form, knowing what you want and realizing that the means for demonstrating it is within your own mind.

2. Activate this emotion of desire by feeling and wanting something with intensity. This emotion transmits electric and magnetic impulses to your central nervous system, impelling you in the direction of that which you desire.

When you desire food, you are driven to seek means to find it. The desire cells that line your stomach walls send little hunger messages to the brain, telling it to furnish the stomach with food. The hunger urge is the strongest urge in man, even stronger than the sex urge.

Your brain also has desire cells—the desire to succeed; the desire to creatively express yourself; the desire to win friends and have their respect and admiration; the desire to make money, and have comfort, security and luxury. You have desire cells of the mind, the body, the heart, and the soul.

Express these inner desires by listing the things you want in your life. Then activate the desire by starting the dynamic creative action that can bring into instant demonstration that which you hold as a mental image.

A woman I once knew had a desire to marry the young man of her choice, and everything was set for the wedding. However, he changed his mind at the last moment and she was left stranded, with the invitations out, her wedding gown bought, and all arrangements made. This shock sent the girl into such a state of bewilderment that she retired from all social life and contemplated suicide. She felt her life was finished.

A friend brought her into our work in Carnegie Hall, and I saw the girl in a private consultation. I listened to her tearful account of what had happened, and how hopeless her life seemed now.

I told her, "You are the same person you were before this terrible thing happened. You still have a natural urge to marry and have a family. You must begin now to build your life on a more solid foundation with the laws of Mind Cosmology."

I then gave her a regime to follow, in which she was to quietly meditate every day on the ideal man she would attract for the future. She was to quietly plan her wedding, to forget the past with its tragic overtones, and realize that she made a mistake, as we all do on occasions, but this was no reason for her to retire from life.

This girl took on a new aura of hope and optimism. She began to live under the laws of Mind Cosmology; she projected the image of love that she hoped to attract, and within three weeks time she met a young attorney who proposed marriage; it was love at first sight for him, and this girl had her beautiful church wedding, and all her relatives and friends were there in triumph, to witness the glorious fulfillment of her dreams.

3. Invoke the cosmic law of magnetic attraction. Your mind has been given the power possessed by a magnet; it can attract into its orbit of action anything that it holds within itself.

Magnetize your brain centers with the idea of riches. See money coming to you from many channels—not just from your work, but from other creative efforts. Project mental energy in visualizing yourself doing the work you want; going into your own business; inventing some useful object; writing songs or stories; making money through investments; taking trips to various parts of the world.

When you magnetize your brain centers with creative ideas, they will set into motion the higher cosmic forces that work through you, releasing the power to achieve every goal that you desire.

A man I once knew lost his job because the company no longer needed his services. He was desolate, for it was a good job and he had been in line for promotion. When he sought my advice, I told him that the same power that had created one opportunity for him was still in existence. Cosmic mind knew his needs. I told him to go into quiet meditation for half an hour each day and ask for divine guidance as to the working out of that financial problem.

Within one week he called me to tell me that another company had heard through a friend of theirs that he was at liberty, and they needed a man with his background and experience to manage a department in a large industrial plant. He got a better job at a bigger salary than he had formerly!

4. Use the cosmic law of subsconscious motivation to stir your creative mind centers into dynamic action.

Your subconscious mind is the connecting link between the superconscious mind and your conscious mind. The superconscious is what gives man his psychic and intuitive guidance. In our study of Mind Cosmology we call this the cosmic mind of God.

To harness this subconscious mind use auto-suggestions that are positive and dynamic.

Each night before going to sleep say the following auto-suggestions at least ten times each, with sincerity:

> I desire a healthy, strong, youthful body with vitality and energy.
> I ask for guidance in solving my problems.
> I want the sum of one thousand (or more) dollars, to pay my bills and give me financial security.
> I desire overcoming the habit of smoking (or any other habit, such as gambling, drinking, etc.).
> I desire psychic and intuitive guidance so I can live a better and more successful life.
> I wish to become rich and successful so I can help my family and the world.
> I desire a better memory so I can remember important things.

Remember—each auto-suggestion should be repeated from

ten to twenty times. Choose four or five only for each night's imprinting, and add as many as you need from time to time.

A movie actress I once knew could not remember her lines; the studios had to write them on a blackboard out of camera range. I gave her this secret of auto-suggestion for a better memory, and within a short time she was able to remember her lines perfectly.

One woman suffered from migraine headaches so badly that she had thought of killing herself. The headaches did not yield to medicines and the doctors told her the pains were due to psychosomatic causes which they could not cure. She began to give herself auto-suggestions that her pains would leave her, that whatever the cause, her subconscious mind would cure her, and within two weeks this woman completely overcame her headaches!

5. Use the cosmic law of imagination to bring your mind new dimensions of creative power.

Someone has called the imagination "God's workshop." It is one of the most powerful forces in the human psyche. Mental imagery sets the autonomic nervous system for action in keeping with that which you imagine.

This law works for good or bad. If you constantly imagine accidents, the reflex action of your nerves and muscles is set for emergencies constantly and creates tension, which might produce the very accidents you want to avoid.

If you set your mental imagery each day on good, happy, healthy, rich experiences, you will project this mental image to the cells of your body, and you will be propelled in the direction of the positive things you imagine.

A woman I once knew could not hold a job. She imagined that everyone in the office disliked her and talked behind her back. Her peculiar reactions did, indeed, cause others to notice her. When I changed her mental images from distrust to trust, from hate to love, from enmity to friendship, this woman underwent a change and soon externalized her mental images in actions that made people like her. She kept her job after that time and won many new friends.

6. Practice the cosmic law of reciprocity daily in your life. This simply means to give something back to the world for that which you receive.

The law of reciprocity generally starts by giving first:

Give smiles and you win friends.

Give service and you will receive money and other rewards.

Give love and consideration and you will have love in return.

Give beauty and you will be rewarded with deep, inner satisfaction.

Give happiness and share your joyous experiences with others, and the world will acclaim you.

A girl who came into our lecture work was a waitress in a little, cheap restaurant. She bewailed the fact she could never rise above her surroundings with the laws of Mind Cosmology. I told her to change her mental attitude; to begin to look and think and act as though she worked in the Waldorf. She was to smile at her customers, stop thinking about the size of tips, and give as good service as though she worked in a high class restaurant. This girl changed her whole appearance after this advice. Within three months time she met a man who wanted to open his own restaurant, and suggested to this girl that she come into the venture with him. He had been impressed by her radiant, joyous attitude. They formed a partnership and this girl is now married, a big success in her own restaurant, and her partner is her husband!

SUMMARY OF CHAPTER SIXTEEN

1. How to invoke cosmic mind power to bring you the things you want in the immediate present and not have to wait years for your demonstration of health, happiness, love, and money.
2. How one young man used Mind Cosmology laws to demonstrate instant success as a composer and got thousands of dollars and a contract with a movie studio.
3. How you can use the law of activated desire to stir the atoms of your brain and project creative action that brings success.
4. How a woman, who had been rejected by her sweetheart,

used Mind Cosmology laws of desire to attract another sweetheart in love and marriage.

5. You can invoke the cosmic law of magnetic attraction and magnetize your brain centers with the idea of riches, new work, travel, friends, health, and happiness.

6. The cosmic law of subconscious motivation and how it can work its miracles of healing and attraction for you.

7. How to use auto-suggestions to your subconscious mind at night before going to sleep to give you a better memory, healing, guidance, and improvement in every department of your life.

8. How a woman used auto-suggestions to overcome the violent pains of migraine headaches when doctors could no longer help her.

9. The cosmic law of imagination to bring your mind new dimensions of creative mind power. How to use it for positive purposes.

10. How a woman used this cosmic law to overcome her suspicion of people and soon won a better job and many friends.

11. The cosmic law of reciprocity and how you can use it to give you money, joy, health, and rich rewards from life.

12. How a waitress used this law of reciprocity and soon met a man who formed a partnership with her in their own restaurant, later marrying this man.

17

How to Motivate the Cosmic Stream of Time for Your Success

You have been given a tremendous power by the cosmic intelligence that created you. You have the ability to motivate and control the cosmic stream of time and bend it to your will. You can accelerate time or slow it down, so that in your youth you can achieve amazing things usually reserved for the latter years. Or if your are old you can turn the cosmic timeclock back and freeze it at any age level you choose, causing you to take on the youthful appearance, vitality and vibrant good health of the young.

Mind Cosmology reveals that time is related to the stream of consciousness and has no relationship to actual time and space as measured on earth.

Einstein's theory of relativity proved that time is relative; it depends on where you are at a specific moment in space, or the rate of vibration which you set up in your brain waves.

185

Some people have accelerated brain wave patterns, which make everything happen very rapidly for them. These brain waves can now be measured by an electroencephalograph and scientists have learned amazing things about the human consciousness and what we call the stream of time.

Other people have a slow brain wave pattern and it takes them longer to learn new things, and time seems to pass slowly for such people. They have delayed success, often in the latter years of their lives; they seldom get new and inspiring creative ideas, and their lives are often dull and routine with very few interesting new experiences or exciting adventures.

You Can Program Your Consciousness to New Dimensions

You have been given the power to program into your higher mind new dimensions of awareness that will give you power to control the time mechanism of the cosmic timeclock.

This cosmic timeclock regulates the length of time in which various events shall occur on the earth plane.

A chick matures in twenty-one days, but it takes nine months for a baby to be fully formed.

This cosmic time clock matures crops in the summer, and they are harvested in the fall.

Many people who have learned this cosmic secret have programmed success in their consciousness to make it occur early in life. They did not have to wait until they were forty or fifty to achieve financial success.

Cosmic mind has programmed you to mature at a certain age, to have certain characteristics, bodily organs and hereditary traits that were programmed into the genes of your mother and father. However, science has now found that we may alter these facts and change the cosmic programming if we choose. To show you how to do this is the purpose of this chapter.

Make Your Success Happen Now!

You can accelerate time and make your success happen now. If you want to achieve some goal that normally might take years, you have the power to accelerate the stream of time flowing through your consciousness and achieve your success immediately.

Science is now able to bombard growing plants with radioactive waves and greatly accelerate their rate of growth, causing them to mature in half the time required by nature.

Giant tomatoes, potatoes and other vegetables, as well as fruit and grains, are now artificially produced by altering their normal vibratory rate of growth.

Enormous chickens and giant rabbits and rats can now be created in the laboratory through changing the genetic patterns of the cells.

A human being, such as Lincoln or Edison, can now be reproduced like a rubber stamp through alterations in the genes of the individual. The facial form and similar characteristics of the individual may be programmed into such a human being and he could be perpetuated forever! This has been done in the laboratory and is no longer theory.

Burbank used this law of motivating cosmic time and design and created new fruits, vegetables and flowers.

You Can Freeze the Stream of Time or Accelerate It

You have been given the power to freeze the stream of time flowing through your consciousness and be young and vital for many years. Or, you can accelerate the stream of time and achieve miraculous things in your life in the eternal now, not having to wait for years for your plans to mature, or to be successful and rich.

I once knew a young man of twenty-two who came into our work. He had only a high school education because his parents were too poor to send him to college. This young man wanted to achieve success while he was still young enough to enjoy it. He learned about these cosmic laws and he decided to accelerate the stream of time and make his success happen in the immediate now.

He sat in meditation each day for an hour, and projected his consciousness into the future dimensions of time and space, using this dynamic affirmation to accelerate the cosmic time clock:

> I wish to attain fame and fortune while I am still young. I now project my cosmic mind power to the age of forty. I desire the wisdom and maturity and experience of that age. I wish to make a fortune and to achieve world-wide recognition. I now accelerate the stream of cosmic time so that my mind becomes mature and my body becomes stabilized at this age. My reasoning and my imaginative faculties are now unlimited.

This young man began to listen to the guiding voice of the cosmic mind, telling him to achieve the objective he had set for himself. He wanted to do something great, but he did not know what. One afternoon, as he sat in meditation, he got an impulse to write a play. He had never studied playwriting, but he had the confidence that he would be guided.

His fingers flew over the keyboard of the typewriter, and in three weeks he had written a comedy, which was produced on Broadway, and ran for three years! It was later made into a movie, bringing him a fortune, and at the age of twenty-six he became a tremendous success in the entertainment world, where he has steadily reaped a fortune running into the millions!

A woman who came to the attention of science, had a terrific shock at the age of twenty when her sweetheart married another girl. This woman's mind became frozen in time and space at the age of twenty and never changed. Her mind had so completely withdrawn from reality that she was no longer aware of the passage of time. All throughout her life, her face and body bore the imprint of youth, and when she died at the age of eighty, scientists performed an autopsy and announced that her body cells, her features, and her organs had actually remained stationary at the age of twenty!

The Regime For Motivating the Cosmic Stream of Time

1. Because time is only an imaginary function of the mind, be

aware in your own mind that time is a moving stream only in your own consciousness. You have seen motion pictures of flowers opening their petals in all their dazzling loveliness in just a few seconds on the screen, but which really took hours in real life. This acceleration of time is done by camera tricks and delayed action photography, but a similar process may be invoked in your own mind, when you know how to motivate the moving stream of time in your consciousness.

2. Sit in periods of imagination and visualize yourself frozen in time and space, at your present age. Visualize time having brought you fame and fortune, fulfillment in love and marriage—see the full-grown family of two or four children. You may set that cosmic timeclock as you wish in this imaginary fourth dimensional plane of imagination.

When you are asleep or under an anesthetic, time becomes frozen for you and never seems to change.

A person frozen for a thousand years would awaken and go on in his consciousness from the moment he left off thinking, and never really know how many centuries had passed.

A person who is drowning often telescopes his entire lifetime into a few seconds of time.

3. Mentally project into the present the future success you desire. Visualize your talents blooming, like a flower, in the eternal now.

Live in your dream house in that imaginary flight into the future dimensions of time and space. See the family you will raise there; entertain your friends; drive in the car you will one day own. As you meditate in this state of consciousness, see and feel that these things are actually happening to you now.

Your brain waves can be accelerated and actually produce these miracles you project in your mind into the eternal now.

How One Man Used This Cosmic Power to Accelerate Time

A man I once taught these cosmic lessons to, desired to make a large fortune so that he could return to his native land and retire. He set his cosmic timeclock to make his fortune in five years time. He asked for the sum of one hundred and fifty thousand dollars in that time. He was then only thirty-five years of age, and had no large sums of money to invest.

This man's wife had been a cosmetologist before they married; they now had three children, and she did not work at her profession, but one day, as she sat in meditation, she got the idea of going back into her work and specializing in the making and selling of wigs. She told her husband of her vision, and he became excited at the possibilities, since wigs were beginning to be the fashion among American women. They opened a small place, soon hired three people and, in six months, moved to a big factory. Now, after only three years, this couple has almost made the entire sum that this man had projected as their retirement fund.

4. Sit before a mirror a few moments a day and give yourself a cosmic mirror treatment. As you look at yourself in the mirror deliberately slow down your brain waves to a very leisurely pace. Do this by saying the following auto-suggestion: "I am now in the cosmic stream of timelessness. I am as young as eternal spring. I now cosmically freeze my consciousness into the eternal now and stop the aging processes of my face and body."

As you say this positive statement, look at your face in the mirror and visualize the lines being removed. To help this process, use your hands to lift your face into the upward contours of youth, especially if you are middle-aged. If you are young, visualize the youthful lines you now possess as being permanently fixed in time and space at your present age, or any age you choose.

As you fix that image of youth, mentally feel, think and act emotionally, as though you are actually that age.

How a Thirty-year-old Pilot Became Twelve Years Old

In the early days of testing planes, a pilot who was thirty years of age had an amazing mystical experience. At the very moment that he broke through the sound barrier and his plane achieved the speed of sound, he glanced up at a mirror above his head and saw his face. To his astonishment, as he accelerated his plane to the speed of sound, his face became that of a young boy of twelve years of age! He went backwards in time and space, and for only a few seconds this image lasted, but he actually saw the youth he had been at twelve.

Actually, scientifically your body cells are never more than two years of age. Your body cells are reborn every two years and you are changing constantly under these laws of cosmic time and space, so why not fix any age level you wish on your brain and body?

Geniuses have this mystical ability to accelerate the rhythm of their brain waves, and they are able to tap other dimensions of time and space and receive high rates of vibration, which reveal to them the secrets of the ages.

5. Crystallize in your mind and body the image of health and youthful vitality which you wish to maintain.

As you study your reflection in the mirror realize that nothing can destroy that mirror image. It remains forever the same. Likewise, the cosmic reality of your soul is permanently fixed in time and space as youthful, healthy, vital, and strong. In the genes and cells of your brain and body, cosmic mind has programmed the life span of two hundred years or more, at this stage of your evolution. Science now says the human heart has been given the power to keep the body functioning perfectly for that length of time.

The thing that causes age and premature death is the belief that the body must become sick, tired and old, and die at three score and ten.

6. Break this negative programming by crystallizing in your mind the thought that your body is the emanation of a spiritual idea from God and that it is intended to perform perfectly as long as you have a purpose for living. Give yourself daily suggestions to overcome fatigue and negative programming:

> I am a spiritual idea. I am fixed in time and space and am eternally young and healthy. My body cells now reflect cosmic life energy and electricity. My immortality is within my soul. I

now release dynamic cosmic power from my soul and it impregnates every atom and cell of my brain and body, infusing it with life, youth, energy, and immortality.

7. Keep the stream of consciousness moving rapidly through your mind by being creatively active every day of your life. Fill your consciousness with new ideas. Each day study, evolve and grow mentally. Concentrate all your mind power on each day's tasks, living in the moment, and fully enjoying every experience of life.

A woman who studied these laws of Mind Cosmology, used this power every day. She was sixty years of age when she started studying. She felt old, unwanted and useless and was waiting to die. I gave her a new Mind Cosmology regime to practice every day.

Each day when she started her activities, she was to sit for five minutes studying herself in the mirror. She was to fix the image of thirty years of age on her mind and body. She was to project that mirror image into some new interests, a new life experience, and even possibly marriage.

She began her meditations and her use of positive suggestions to reach her higher mind centers. Soon this woman experienced a feeling of well-being and overcame her periods of moodiness and depression. As she contemplated the idea of another marriage, she later told me, she felt like a young girl in the first flush of romance. She was told by a friend of a dance given for middle-aged people at some club every week. She began going to these dances and she met interesting people who were once again finding the joy of living. After two months time she met a retired city councilman there who proposed marriage and she accepted him. Since that time her life has taken on new meaning and purpose.

8. If you feel that time is moving too rapidly, as the aging often do, and you want to slow down the cosmic stream of time, you can do so.

Remember when you were a child waiting for Christmas to come, how long the days seemed? This was because you were closely examining each moment, anxious for it to pass, so you could get to that momentous day you had waited for all year.

Use the same cosmic technique if you wish to prolong an ecstasy, or an emotion, such as love, or some joyous remembrance of past events. Sit quietly in meditation and hold that event in focus in the forefront of your mind. Let your mind dwell on its every facet until you have permanently fixed it in consciousness. This process will slow down the brain waves and make the stream of consciousness move slowly, and as time is nothing more than consciousness, you will seem to live forever in your normal life span.

9. To slow time down and give yourself a feeling of leisure and a richer life experience, fix a very heavy schedule for yourself in your daily activities. Fill your mind with interesting thoughts, study new subjects, learn a foreign language, have a heavy social schedule in which you crowd your life with activity. Have many goals for the future that you want to achieve. Each day program into your mind the limitless concept of your life span, that your soul will live forever, journeying to many planes of consciousness. Realize that this lifetime is only a speck of time in the cosmic seas of eternity.

To give you a concept of what cosmic time and eternity are, concentrate on this concept given by H.G. Wells. He said that if a tiny bird were to come and sharpen its beak on the rock of Gibraltar once every million years, the length of time it would take to wear down the rock of Gibraltar would be eternity.

10. A mystic secret that comes to us from the Far East, that will help you also in slowing down cosmic time, is to use the mystic exercise of contemplation.

Sit in meditation each day and contemplate for half an hour on the mind and its functions. Examine memory, visualization, imagination, subconscious and superconscious minds, until you have a sense of rhythm which slows down your mind, body functions, and heart beat to the rhythm of the cosmic soul.

11. The next day contemplate on the body and its functions. Mentally examine all the body organs and their perfect rhythm. Tune yourself to that rhythm and be aware of the five senses—taste, touch, smell, sight, and hearing. Then intensify

these senses by exercising them and being aware of the outer world through these five senses.

12. The next day contemplate the mystery of creation; examine the mystery of the soul; the purpose of life; the nature of God, until you go into a deep transcendental state of awareness where your higher psychic mind centers are opened and your third eye, the psychic center, is fully aroused and gives you the answers to many of life's baffling mysteries.

SUMMARY OF CHAPTER SEVENTEEN

1. The amazing power you possess to accelerate or slow down the cosmic stream of time and the use of it to achieve amazing things in your life cycles.

2. How you can program your consciousness to new dimensions of time and space and gain control of the mechanism known as the cosmic timeclock.

3. You can make your success happen now, by using a mystic secret from the Far East. You can bring fame, fortune, and power into focus in the eternal now and not have to wait until late in life.

4. How you can freeze the stream of time or accelerate it at will, and mature your mind when young; or slow down the aging processes when old.

5. How a twenty-two-year-old man used this power to accelerate time, wrote a successful play that ran on Broadway for three years, and became one of our most successful playwrights.

6. How a woman at age twenty froze time and maintained the image of youth until the day of her death, never changing for sixty years.

7. How to mentally project into the present the future success you desire by using the power of mind to visualize your future as being already revealed and created in the eternal now.

8. How one man and his wife accelerated cosmic time and went into a business that made them almost one hundred and fifty thousand dollars in three years time.

9. The cosmic mirror treatment to fix time and achieve a youth-

ful mind and body, without aging perceptibly as you grow older.

10. You can crystallize in your mind and body the image of health and youthful vitality, which will keep you young and healthy for one hundred years or more.

11. How to break negative programming of age, sickness, and fatigue by giving yourself daily, positive cosmic-mind programming.

12. How a sixty-year-old woman used this method to program a new, more youthful body and face, and how it won her a proposal of marriage after only two months time.

13. How you can slow down the stream of cosmic time and enjoy every life experience more fully before you go on into the dimensions of the future.

14. The mystic secret of contemplation which can put you into the cosmic rhythm of the soul of the universe, bringing you spiritual awareness and an expanded consciousness.

18

How to Use Cosmo-Astral
Rays for
Healthful Living

There are certain people in India, China and Tibet who have reached such a state of spiritual proficiency in the healing arts that they are able to instantly heal sick bodies, repair torn or burned tissues, and otherwise perform miracles that astound western medical science.

I have seen these holy men walk over red hot coals with bare feet and have examined their feet afterwards. I found no evidence of burned flesh. This amazing feat is performed by them by achieving a trance-like state in which they draw on cosmo-astral forces that cause their bodies to be impervious to injury.

These cosmo-astral rays exist in the atmosphere all about us. They may be tapped by anyone who learns how to use Mind Cosmology to channel the higher, invisible forces that radiate from the cosmic mind man calls God.

In this chapter we shall study these cosmic and astral rays, vibrations, and colors, and learn how to use them for your benefit.

The Mysterious Healing Properties of Radium

We can see how these cosmo-astral rays work in performing their miracle healing in the instance of the natural property called radium. This substance, discovered by the Curies, gave to science an amazing material that glowed in the dark and which gave off mysterious vibrations that can heal cancerous tissue.

We see the mysterious cosmic property known as magnetism, and how it works in nature to hold the planets in their orbits, exerting such power that it motivates billions of tons of water in the ebb and flow of the tides. When you realize how this astral force emanates from the moon that is nearly two hundred and fifty thousand miles from the earth, you will realize how powerful are these mysterious and invisible cosmo-astral forces in their effect on earth and human destiny.

We see this cosmo-astral life energy flowing earthward from the dynamo of the sun and other planets, causing seed in the earth to sprout and grow, giving us their crops in abundance every summer.

Realize that your body is physical and is also motivated by this cosmo-astral energy that emanates from the planetary systems. But behind your physical body is an astral body, which is not subject to the same physical and material laws that govern your physical body. This etheric, spiritual double is the real you; the permanent, indestructible self that operates on the fourth dimensional plane of spirit. This astral self is subject to laws that exist in the invisible as wave lengths or vibrations.

When you wish to conduct healing power from the cosmic dynamo of life energy, you must utilize your higher psychic powers to invoke this life force and conduct it to the cells of your brain and body.

How Jesus Used These Cosmo-Astral Rays
for Miracle Healing

When the Master Metaphysician Jesus wished to perform His miracles of healing, he aroused the higher psychic centers of the sick, causing them to release miracle-working cosmic forces which did the actual work of instantaneous healing. The sick person actually healed himself. Jesus was merely the instrument through which the higher spiritual forces were released.

The Master gave this formula for healing in Mark 11:24—"What things soever ye desire, when ye pray, believe that ye receive them, and ye shall have them."

He summed this up further by saying, "If thou canst believe; All things are possible to him that believeth."

Truly, mankind has entered a fourth dimensional world of cosmic power where it has literally performed miracles with its faith. The end is not yet in sight, for the Master promised, in John 14:12—"Verily, verily, I say unto you, He that believeth on me the works that I do shall ye do also. And greater works than these shall ye do."

The Age of Miracles Has Come to Earth

See how accurate was this prophecy by the Master Jesus.

Man harnessed these cosmo-astral wave lengths of magnetism and flew to the moon, landed and returned to earth safely.

Man created his electronic microscope and can now see into the invisible world, where creatures exist on a minute scale, that are not evident to the normal vision.

Man has tapped the cosmo-astral wave lengths and filled the air with the miracle of sounds, music, colored pictures, that can be projected into a hundred million homes simultaneously on television screens. Truly, a miracle greater than anything the world has ever seen in the past!

Now you may tap these same cosmo-astral spiritual wave lengths and know secrets of the universe. You can tap this higher power and have psychic perception. You may have extra sensory perception, the gift of clairvoyant vision, of precognition and astral flight.

You can know your future, read the thoughts of others, and predict the pattern of events for years to come. You may know secrets of the soul, of the origin and nature of God and other mysteries of creation that previously have been reserved only for mystics, seers, prophets and holy men.

> *How far shall man's questing soul ascend,*
> *Upon that mystic strand that has no end:*
> *But bidding all fair earth adieu:*
> *Nobler, grander vistas come into view.*

So too, when your mind and soul tap these invisible rays of cosmo-astral power, you may truly achieve a miracle-working power that can heal the physical body and perform miracles in every department of your life.

The Regime for Tapping Cosmo-Astral Miracle Working Powers

1. When you wish to channel these higher cosmo-astral rays to your mind and body, sit quietly in meditation for at least a half hour each day. Relax your mind and body; you may lie down or sit in a comfortable chair, with your hands folded in your lap and your eyes closed.

2. Breathe deeply for ten times and say the mystic phrase from Tibet, *Ohm, mane padme ohm.* This helps open the third eye center, which gives psychic vision and literally means, "The jewel in the heart of the lotus," referring to the sacred flower of the Far East as the spiritual center of man's being.

3. Then focus your mind on the astral colors, which represent different astral rays that stream earthward from the cosmic rainbow of God's eternal presence.

4. Fix the astral ray of healing light in your consciousness; take the color mauve, and visualize this first ray as being the high spiritual astral light of high inspiration and spiritual power.

As you hold this astral ray in your consciousness, give your mind a positive cosmic affirmation, directing this healing light to the various organs of your body, saying the following healing affirmation:

> I now am in the consciousness of my eternal, true spiritual identity. My astral body is now being treated for perfect health. My etheric image reflects permanent youth and beauty. My inner soul qualities are now revealed in my body. These soul qualities are the astral forces of peace, youth, beauty, vitality, health, energy, power, dynamic magnetism and divine love.

5. As you hold each of these astral forces in your consciousness, treat the entire body with each one for about three minutes. As you affirm youth, visualize yourself standing in a spotlight of etheral blue, and see this cosmic astral color bathing your body cells with the life-giving cosmic power of youth.

6. As you hold the astral ray of beauty in consciousness, breathe deeply and project the astral ray of white light to your mind and body centers. White, being the pure beam of spiritual light, contains in its ray all the colors of the rainbow. Now affirm:

> I now fix forever in my consciousness the astral ray of white light, which bathes my mind, body and soul in its healing, beauteous color. I reflect beauty in my thoughts, I express beauty in my words and conduct. I inspire beauty in others by radiating the pure white light of truth, goodness, understanding and love.

How a Woman Made Herself Radiantly Lovely with This Cosmic Ray of Beauty

I knew a woman who was rather plain of face and figure who wanted to be attractive to members of the opposite sex. She was already past thirty years of age and was called an old maid by her friends. When she learned about this power of projecting beauty through the etheric image, she began to practice it each day, holding in her moments of meditation the loveliest images she could think. She visualized springtime, with its myriad flowers, multi-colored and waving gracefully in the breeze. She created a mental and spiritual empathy with those fragrant blooms, and when she walked she visualized their grace and rhythm; when she talked, she projected the visual cosmic image of beauty and splendor held by the perfection of a rose; she never allowed her mind to sink into realms of despair and moodiness.

She affirmed each day when she awakened: "I am now in tune with beauty, joy and love, and my etheric self will reflect these qualities in my aura all day. To everyone I meet I shall project the golden ray of divine love and in turn, receive from them, the same divine emotion."

This cosmo astral projection worked miracles for this woman. I met her again three weeks after our first interview and I was amazed at the change in her. She carried her head as though wearing an invisible crown. Her face was ethereal in its expression, as though she held a precious secret deep within her mind. Her voice had changed and was soft and mellow, and caressed each word with love.

This woman attracted a very handsome man, an officer in the army, who was impressed by her dignity, inner radiance and charm. He proposed marriage and she is now entertaining important people in her gracious home in Washington, D.C.

7. To achieve physical healing of the body through these cosmo-astral rays, use the vibrant cosmic ray of red. When you go into meditation to release healing power from the cosmic mind centers, hold in your mind the cosmic ray of red light. Feel that this ray is bathing your body cells in its lifegiving force.

If you can, use a red bulb for purposes of meditation. This bulb, giving off its stimulating, vibrant life force, will help stimulate the psycho-neural centers of your mind, releasing healing vibrations.

Too much red in interior decorating can irritate the nervous system, just as red will cause a bull to charge. But a few moments concentration on this healing ray has salutary effects on the body's health.

8. The astral ray of purple is also a very stimulating color to use for brief periods of meditation. However, scientists found that when a person is exposed for several hours to the vibrations of a purple light, he develops psychotic symptoms, so purple should be used sparingly for meditation. There is no danger of over-stimulation however, in wearing purple shades.

9. Use various shades of green in meditation when you desire healing or a sedative effect for the nerves. You can expose yourself to an electric light bulb of green, and look at it, or you can meditate, with your eyes closed, visualizing the green in nature. There is more green than any other color in the realm of nature, for this is the cosmic healing and relaxing color.

In modern hospitals the walls are now painted shades of light green; even the surgical gowns of doctors are of this color. They have found that green gives off soothing, relaxing and healing vibrations. In most mental hospitals this color has replaced the glaring white that was formerly used.

Project this ray of green to your brain centers, and see it having a calming, sedative effect on your nervous system. Wear green in your costumes, if possible, for it gives off vibrations that are calming and peaceful.

10. The colors of sunlight yellow and orange are to be concentrated on for stimulation of the higher brain centers. These colors should be used in meditation for dissolving problems, making money, or handling business affairs. They are also to be used to stimulate the creative mind centers for art, music, and literature. In meditation, see the creative ray of different shades of yellow and orange whenever you want mild stimulation.

11. Avoid shades of deep blue or black in meditation. The higher mind centers are depressed by this negative polarity of the cosmic spectrum. Light blue and various shades of azure, cerulean, electric blue, and ultramarine blue, are beneficial in their effects and have a mildly sedative effect. The lighter blues are spiritual in their effects and should be used for meditation when trying to develop the psychic centers.

12. The earth colors of brown, yellow ochre, burnt sienna, and indigo, have been found to have a depressing vibration. Avoid using these astral rays in meditation. They are all right in articles of clothing, for they do not exert a powerful effect on the body; only when used in meditation do they tend to depress the nerve and psychic centers.

13. When treating the various mind and body centers with these cosmo-astral vibrations of color, use a powerful cosmic affirmation which you repeat for each light ray that you use:

> I now project the cosmic ray of golden light to heal and energize my body. I am now healed of all disturbances.
> I now project the cosmic ray of red, giving my mind and body stimulating energy, and health and vitality.
> I now project the soothing ray of vibrant cosmic green, calming my nerves and bringing me peace and tranquility.
> I now project the stimulating, spiritual ray of ethereal blue, arousing my higher spiritual perception and focusing power in my higher psychic centers.
> I now project the pure cosmic ray of white light, giving me spiritual power, and releasing all the cosmic colors of the rainbow in my mind, body and soul. I now blend with the pure white light of truth and am in the center of cosmic power, life and intelligence.

SUMMARY OF CHAPTER EIGHTEEN

1. The miracles performed by the holy men and Yogas of India in healing the sick body and performing feats such as walking on hot coals without harm.

2. How these cosmo-astral invisible rays work in the realm of nature, releasing magnetism which is the secret power back of life.

3. How the Master Jesus used these cosmo-astral rays for achieving His miracles of healing, and gave mankind the mystical formula for doing even greater works than those performed by Him.

4. How mankind has begun to use these miracle working powers

in his electronic microscope, his radio, television and space ships, defying the laws of gravity to achieve miracles.

5. You can tap these cosmo-astral wave lengths to know secrets of the universe; to have psychic guidance, to be able to know the future—this power is available for performing miracles.

6. The cosmic regime for achieving this miracle working power by concentrating and meditating on the astral rays of light that exist in the invisible universe.

7. The astral cosmic rays of peace, youth, beauty, health, vitality, energy, power, magnetism and love, that you may tap in channeling miracle-working cosmo-astral healing rays.

8. The cosmo-astral rays of light and how to use cosmic colors as therapy to help shape your mind and body.

9. How to treat the mind and body centers with these cosmo-astral rays of color, and use the positive vibrations of affirmations for all purposes.

19

How Cosmology Can Magnetize, Attract and Hold Your Desired Mate

You were created to know and experience true love. For every person there is a true soul mate. When you once learn how to use the laws of Mind Cosmology, you can magnetize and attract your true soul mate in love and marriage. No matter what your age, love is the indispensable element that can make your life complete.

As Browning said: "Take away love and the earth is a tomb."

In this chapter you will learn how to magnetize and attract into the orbit of your life experience the mate who will respond to your love magnetically and emotionally and be the perfect mate for you.

In this modern age where the attitude towards love has become somewhat cynical and permissive, people are no longer able to share their life experience with one person. Three out of five marriages end in divorce. This has led to a feeling of insecurity in the lives of millions of children, as well as a hopelessness among adults, giving them a pessimistic philosophy, which profoundly affects their lives in every department.

Why Mrs. Rita L. Had Chronic Fatigue and Headaches

A woman came into our lecture work in Carnegie Hall, and told me she had continual fatigue, headaches, and a general feeling of debility. She said, "I feel that something awful is going to happen and I am powerless to stop it."

I then learned that she was married and had two children, but had separated from her husband because he had been going around with another woman.

Rita L. still loved her husband, and she was now living without love and an outlet for her deep emotions. The husband came to see the children frequently and there had been no talk of a divorce.

I told Rita L. that she must make an attempt to heal the broken marriage, but she complained, "How can I take him back when I know he's been with another woman?"

Then I gave Rita L. the Mind Cosmology regime for winning and holding true love, which would guarantee that her husband, when he once returned to her, would never leave her for another woman.

This regime included these five points:

1. To forgive her husband and take him back for the sake of their children, and to never mention again her jealousy or suspicion, but act as though she trusted him implicitly.

2. She was to completely restyle her self-image from an ordinary housewife into one of glamour, beauty and magnetism, through a regime which I gave her, and which we shall discuss later in this chapter.

3. She was to practice the art of expressing love not only in a physical relationship, but on a mental and spiritual plane as well. She was to see her husband as her true soul mate, the father of her two wonderful children, and as the man God intended to be her mate for life.

4. She was to mentally weave a spell of romance and beauty over her husband's mind, by creating the atmosphere for perpetual love in her mind, and in her home. She was to prepare herself for his arrival each night from work, and be ready to join him in his various experiences and needs, and not be so exhausted from housework that her husband became a secondary interest in her life.

5. She was to break the negative mesmerism of the drudgery of her daily life by going out more often, finding ways to leave the children with a responsible person, while she danced, went to movies, or shared in bowling or other activities that could bring her and her husband into a closer partnership and friendship.

Rita L. began working on this program of Mind Cosmology. She took her husband back after he told her he did not love the other woman but that it was only a temporary affair. She began to build the new self-image of love and romance in her home, and soon she and her husband were in a more loving and harmonious relationship than they had been in all the five years of previous marriage. Now, three years later, I still hear from Rita L. and love has lasted, bringing her every joy she had expected from life.

The Regime for Attracting and Magnetizing
Your Soul Mate

1. Attune your mind to the glorious harmony of love. Just as a musician must tune his violin to make sweet music, so too your mind and heart and soul must be daily attuned to the divine chord of love.

Each day, when you start your day, give yourself a magnetic suggestion: "All day I shall be attuned to the high vibrations of love. My thoughts, words and acts shall be loving. I shall do nothing today that reflects jealousy, suspicion, animosity or hate. I am charged with the vibrations of God's divine romance and I shall so conduct myself all day."

2. Magnetize your mind centers with the vibrations of

spiritual love by reading beautiful love poetry and reciting poems,until you have captured the beauty and spirit of spiritual love. The poems of Elizabeth Barrett Browning are specially suited to this purpose. The poem, "How do I Love Thee?" should be memorized by every person who wishes to capture the spirit of love forevermore in his heart.

The magnificent poetry of Shakespeare in his *Venus and Adonis,* is also to be read and enthroned in consciousness. Poetry often reflects more than anything else the cosmic spirit of divine love.

3. Practice each day releasing the emotion of love on all planes of consciousness. Love is more than a physical attraction between two people; it is a mental and spiritual expression as well. Learn to attune your mind to that of the beloved, hold similar interests, study things together, plan events that you may share, so you build a unity of interests that binds you together on more than one plane of expression. Most young people make the mistake of falling in love with the physical person, and they fail to see the spiritual person behind the material facade of life.

A woman who made this mistake married a man who was handsome, a football hero in his school, had a full, beautiful head of hair, and a figure like a Grecian god. She fell in love with this man physically, and married him impetuously. But when she was married a year she found that the man was not romantic, was rude and unkind and showed such bad manners that she regretted having married him. She had a child in that first year of marriage, and for the sake of the baby girl she stayed with her husband. In the third year they had another child, a little boy, but her husband did not improve. He began staying out late nights; she suspected he was seeing another woman, and she became disenchanted with him. Not only that, but he was losing his hair, had become overweight and lost his perfect athletic build, which had really attracted her in the first place.

This woman came into Mind Cosmology in the fifth year of her marriage, told me her sad story of disillusionment and asked frantically, "What can I do now? I want a divorce but what will become of our children?"

I knew that divorce was not the answer, and I also knew that the woman alone could produce the change that was needed to turn this disaster into a happy marriage. I advised her to bring her husband to our lectures and also for personal counselling, for I suspected that the fault was more his than that of his wife.

The man did come to the lectures and for personal counselling. I started him on a Mind Cosmology regime which he was to rigidly follow; in fact, the program included certain mental exercises which the husband and wife were to practice together.

They were once more to build common interests.

The wife was to stop looking at the physical man she had married when he was younger and more athletic, and to begin to see the inner man that he was now trying to become.

He was given a regime of diet and exercise which would once again bring him back to his former physical appearance.

The wife was told to forgive him if he was having an affair with another woman, and to win back his love by being loving, kind, and considerate.

They were both to go on a short honeymoon, leaving their children with relatives, and to act as though this were the real honeymoon. They were to recapture the spirit of love once more, and begin to feel the magnetism and attraction of their earlier relationship.

Their personal Mind Cosmology romantic program included much more, incorporating many of the points which we shall cover in this chapter.

I observed this couple for a period of two years, during which they came once a week to my lectures in Carnegie Hall. They began to change miraculously. He began to be more considerate, he refined his personality, and began to be more romantic and solicitous of his wife's happiness. Soon he had kindled the romantic spark in his wife once more and they were as close, if not closer, than before, but now their relationship was not just physical—it was mental and spiritual as well as physical. This home was kept intact and this couple is now experiencing greater joy than they had ever thought possible in love and marriage.

4. The law of romantic attraction in Mind Cosmology decrees that like attracts like. You can only attract the true soul mate when you both vibrate on the same plane of consciousness.

Mentally select the mental and spiritual qualities you desire in a mate. Write these down on a romantic chart. Put down a physical description of the mate first, then make out a list of the mental qualities you desire. Your list, if you are a man, might look like this:

> I desire a woman who is of medium height, slender, with grace and charm. Blonde hair, blue eyes; even, regular features. I want the following qualities in my future wife:
>
> She is to be kind and gentle, having consideration for others.
>
> She should be unselfish and desire a loving husband, a good home, and a family of two or three children.
>
> I want a wife who will be a good hostess in the home; one who will be interested in music, art and good books. A woman who enjoys athletic events and can share with me my interest in all sports.
>
> I want a wife with a good home background, from a family where there was love and unity, and a spiritual background and good, sound moral values.

5. If a woman, you can make out the romantic chart with the specifications you desire in a future soul mate. The reason you must know what these qualities are, is that you cannot attract such a person unless you vibrate to the same level of mental and spiritual inspiration.

6. Do not merely look at the physical being, but check on character, qualities of honesty and integrity; a mate who is concerned about other people; one who believes in God and is of the same religious faith as yourself.

7. There are eight stages of romantic ecstasy which can be built between any loving couple. When these are established in the relationship, nothing can shatter such a union:

> A. You will enjoy doing the same things; you will have

the same interest in hobbies, sports, social activities and you will enjoy the same type of books, music and art.

B. You will both operate on the same plane of high moral standards of honesty, goodness, truth, charity and idealism.

C. You will both be repelled by vulgarity, lying, cheating, stealing, immoral conduct, and infractions of the Ten Commandments. You will share a desire to idealize yourselves and build perfection in mind and body.

D. You will have so much magnetism between each other that you will want to be together constantly sharing the same emotions, friends, experiences and entertainments.

E. You will respond emotionally to the same high standards of beauty in art, music, literature. You will share the enjoyment of the wonders of nature, building similar interests in sports and outdoor activities that are healthful and enjoyable.

F. You will magnetize and attract a circle of friends who have your interests, similar personalities, and basically enjoy the same type of humor and conversation.

G. In this romantic relationship you will have an unselfish desire to share all your wonderful experiences with your beloved. This includes all your good fortune, your money, your secrets, your ideas and ideals, never excluding your mate from the bonds of intimacy and personal relationship.

H. You will create strong bonds of physical and sexual love, that will outlast the first magnetic attraction which might have been physical. You will add, as you grow older, the spiritual type of love that will encompass not only your family but God and the world.

8. Learn to weave a spell of romantic entrancement about the mind and heart of the beloved. This is done by mentally projecting the thoughts of love, beauty and goodness that you want to lodge in the mind and soul of the soul mate. Each night, when you go to sleep, look at a photograph of the person

you want to marry; or if you do not have a photograph, hold the person's face in the forefront of your mind. Then talk to that astral image; weave your romantic spell of entrancement with the following words:

> I project my loving thoughts to you before going to sleep. I love you and I believe you are my true soul mate. If it is God's will, we shall be together for an eternity. I want to share with you every beautiful and loving experience I have in my future. I ask that you respond to my love with the same emotion and intensity I now feel. I caress you, and in my heart and soul, I know that God intended for us to marry and have a beautiful family. You will sense this magnetic projection and will respond with love.

How a Girl Used This Ritual to Win an "Impossible" Love

A girl of only twenty came to my attention in New York, where I was lecturing on Mind Cosmology. She told me a sad story; she was in love with a young man who was twenty-four. He was of a different faith, and although his family admired her, for she was from a good family, they had other plans for their son. They wanted him to finish his education and become a surgeon, like his father. Then they wanted him to marry a girl, of the same faith, whom they had already selected. This family was quite wealthy and they wanted their son to marry into a family where there was considerable wealth.

The boy had been going with this girl for six months and was deeply in love with her, but when he told his family, they held a conference and decided he was to go away to college immediately, break off with the girl and never see her again.

When the girl told me this, she said she felt that she would have to give up this boy, for she would not go against his family.

However, I told her if she really loved him, that was all that really mattered. After all, it was the boy's life, not his family's.

I gave her a regime to work on mentally and spiritually. She did not see the boy again, for he was in Boston, studying at a big college there, but she had his photograph. I told her to look at that picture every night before going to bed; to feel the boy was there in the room with her. "Time and distance are no barriers to thought waves," I told her. "Project the desire you have to marry this boy. Tell him how you love him. Ask him to make up his own mind, and to telephone you when he feels sure he really loves you and wants to marry you."

This girl kept up this projection of her romantic thought waves for two weeks, at the same time imagining herself married. She was to project the actual wedding; she was to look at bridal dresses, choose hers, visualize herself walking down the aisle holding her father's arm as he gave her away. She was even to visualize the honeymoon, the beautiful romantic events preceding and after, and the establishing of their home together.

Within two weeks time this girl received a letter from the boy. He told her, "I had a vivid dream of you dressed in a bridal veil in a church ceremony, in which we became husband and wife. I know now that I love you and I am coming to New York to ask you to be my wife."

The amazing thing about this projection of love by this girl was that it was so vivid that the boy's family finally consented, the wedding was arranged, and this blissful couple were soon on their honeymoon, exactly as the girl had projected it in her mental images!

SUMMARY OF CHAPTER NINETEEN

1. How to use the laws of Mind Cosmology to magnetize and attract your true soul mate in a union that will last forever.

2. How Mrs. Rita L. overcame a disastrous marriage which had made her physically ill, and was able to overcome every problem and win back her husband's love and adoration in a marriage that became more wonderful than ever.

3. How to attune your mind to the glorious harmony of love, and achieve the attraction of someone who is magnetically attracted to you.

4. How to use beautiful poetry to increase romantic feelings,

and inspire the ideal of love in the mind and heart of your beloved.

5. How to know all facets of love and not live merely for physical or sexual love, but by building unity of interests.

6. How one woman made the mistake of falling in love on the physical plane alone, and how it nearly destroyed her life. She overcame this and went on to happiness through a Mind Cosmology regime given her.

7. How to invoke the magnetic law of attraction which states, "Like attracts like," and build vibrations on the same plane of consciousness of your soul mate.

8. How to create your own personal romantic chart through Mind Cosmology principles, in which you project the mental, physical and spiritual qualities you want in your soul mate.

9. The eight stages of romantic ecstasy which you can build, and create a romantic relationship that nothing can ever shatter.

10. How to create bonds of physical and sexual love that will outlast the first magnetic attraction and yield later to a deep spiritual form of love that is eternal.

11. How to weave a spell of romantic entrancement about the mind and heart of your beloved by projecting the mental images of love, beauty and goodness that you want in your beloved.

12. How a girl of twenty used this ritual to win an impossible love, where the boy's parents opposed the union. She won out over all opposition and went on to a brilliant and happy marriage.

20

How to Know Your
Ultimate Destiny
Through Cosmology

Your soul has embarked upon a mystical journey in time and space that will eventually lead you to the finding of your ultimate cosmic destiny. Your soul is the communicating medium with the higher cosmic mind that knows all secrets and which can lead you to the fulfillment of your every dream.

This chapter will help you explore the mystery of the human soul and show you how to use Mind Cosmology so you may achieve Darshan, the mystic term in ancient Sanskrit for ultimate cosmic fulfillment.

The spiritual reality of man has been proven over and over. Man knows with an intuitive knowledge that he has experienced certain spiritual experiences, which are of the soul, not the mind or body. But for the first time in this century, proof of the soul's true existence was given by scientists in Paris, France. At the exact moment of a man's death, he was weighed on

215

scales and it was found that as he expired there was a perceptible loss of several ounces of body weight when his soul left his physical body.

For centuries mystics and seers have taught that the celestial journey of the soul is a reality. It seeks out its life experiences for a purpose. You were sent onto this earth plane for a divine mission and when your soul awareness is increased to a point of cosmic consciousness, you know your future and are able to fulfill it.

The Mystical Properties of Your Soul

The soul has the ability to communicate with other souls, on invisible wave lengths that are in the fourth dimensional plane. You can tap these spiritual wave lengths with your own soul's perception, just as a modern television set can bring on its screen the pictures that are in the invisible.

"Soul speaks to soul, as star to star."

Your soul has this amazing ability to communicate with others on invisible spiritual wave lengths, while you sleep.

Your soul can be projected out into time and space, and examine past periods of history in astral projection.

Your astral self, the soul's radiation, may actually be seen by people, many times in what appear to be dreams, and sometimes in actual daylight, when they are wide awake.

The great mystic St. Germain actually materialized as an astral soul projection to three of his disciples at the same time. They saw his astral self, and it appeared as real as his solid, physical body.

To better grasp what the soul is and how it can permeate matter, consider the following analogy—water is a fluid substance, but when it is frozen, it becomes solid; then the ice can be melted by heat and it becomes steam, once again condensing as the fluid water.

So too, the soul is a permeating intelligence that has the power to manifest in the human body as spirit. The body is analogous to the frozen state of water, and is like the ice. The steam is the intelligence of cosmic mind that permeates the

brain and body; the water is analogous to the human consciousness or mind with its various aspects of awareness.

How to Use the Soul's Mystic Properties to Achieve
Cosmic Fulfillment

1. Cosmic consciousness may be achieved when your soul
releases its knowledge and power to your conscious mind. You
may then use this knowledge to achieve the greatness that
should be your true destiny.

Make it a point to abide by the spiritual laws that have been
released to the world by the great mystics, teachers and
prophets of the past. Moses released the cosmic laws known as
the Ten Commandments. You must abide by these great
spiritual laws, and your soul will be given a further impetus to
cosmic enlightenment.

The great Mystic Jesus revealed the Sermon on the Mount
with its cosmic Golden Rule. When you live by these cosmic
laws, you achieve release of true soul power.

Another great cosmic law was released by the Master. He
said, "A New commandment I give unto you; that ye love one
another." So love becomes a cosmic law pertaining to the heart
and soul of man, and displaced the old Mosaic Law, "An eye for
an eye and a tooth for a tooth," which prevailed back in the old
days of revenge and justice on an individual basis.

How Mr. T. L. Violated the Cosmic Law and Suffered
a Breakdown in Health

Mr. T. L. came into my lecture work in New York City,
suffering from high blood pressure, heart trouble and ulcers. He
was a very sick man and the doctors had given him up, and told
him he did not have too long to live.

Out of desperation T. L. turned to a study of Mind Cosmology to find out how he might save himself. He was only
forty-five years of age, had a fine wife and two beautiful
daughters of marriageable age. He wanted to live some years
longer to help his family achieve security.

In my first interview with him I discovered the secret cause of all his mental and physical afflictions. He had been in business with his brother, and they should have made a fortune, but the business seemed to be constantly losing money. Finally T. L. investigated the books and found that his brother had been siphoning all the money off into his own pockets, thus bringing about the collapse of the business.

T. L. hated his brother from that moment on. He had to start all over again to build his business, but his health rapidly deteriorated, and he developed symptoms which the doctors could not understand. Finally, after five years of still holding hatred in his heart, he came to me for help.

I immediately put T. L. on a Mind Cosmology regime, which was to first forgive his brother for what had happened. His hatred was making him mentally and physically sick.

After he did this he said he felt as if a great weight had been lifted off his heart. Then he was to begin doing certain exercises each day which would put his soul into attunement with the cosmic soul of the universe; he was to do good for others; he was to spend at least one hour a day in meditation and clear his mind of all thoughts of hate, fear, worry, or revenge. He then started doing better work, his business prospered, and amazingly enough, in six months' time most of his symptoms of sickness disappeared! He is now on the road to complete recovery and has learned his great cosmic lesson.

2. The mystic progress of your immortal soul through this valley of material reality depends on your knowledge of the laws pertaining to the soul's progress and evolution.

The soul is ever striving onwards and upwards in the shadow-filled valleys of mortal mind fear, problems, sickness, age and death, until it sees the beginning rays of spiritual light dawning on the unlimited horizons of the mind and spirit. The soul struggles constantly towards the light of God's ultimate reality, which the ancients called Nirvana.

3. The first stage of soul enlightenment is to sit quietly in meditation and practice the mystic process of mindfulness.

Be aware of this higher spiritual and cosmic power that you possess within your soul. Your soul has issued forth from the crucible of time, knowing all secrets, having seen the splendor of God's countenance. But when your soul becomes clothed in its fleshy body, it often cannot communicate its higher visions, dreams and aspirations to the conscious mind. The conscious mind has been programmed with all kinds of earthly and materialistic concepts.

4. Clear this consciousness of all negative, false concepts that have been put into your conscious mind. Remove the dark clouds of doubt, skepticism, fear, hate and worry, so that the clear light of cosmic truth may shine through your higher psychic sensors, giving you inner illumination and guidance for the future events or your life.

5. To gain a clearer understanding of how to remove these mortal mind clouds of negativity, take a clear glass of water and drop a pinch of dirt into it. See how the water becomes cloudy and loses its transparency? Now let the mud settle to the bottom of the glass and once again the water is clear. So too, your consciousness is the same way; when the mortal dust of fear, worry, hate, jealousy, greed and selfishness cloud the consciousness, the higher psychic centers through which your soul projects its cosmic blueprint of destiny, become clouded and cannot accurately see the glorious visions it has within its mystical realm.

A woman who had lived a life of discord, friction and negativity came into our lecture work and told me how she had lost her husband's love; she was sick, tired and discouraged. She told me she had hated her husband for years before they were divorced, because she discovered he had been untrue to her. Instead of forgiving him and going on to a better life, she had let hate, jealousy and suspicion curdle within her, until it shattered her marriage and broke her health. Her three children, now all grown, had deserted her and she was alone and bitter.

Here was a typical case of how mortal mind clouds can dim the soul's true splendor and keep us earth-bound and miserable. I gave this woman a positive affirmation she was to use every day to clear her consciousness of hatred and bitterness as follows:

I am now in the center of cosmic consciousness. I am aware of knowing and I am a channel for cosmic mind to work through me. I am aware of my mortal mind limitations. I now purify my mind of all clouds of hate, fear, worry, and other negative emotions. Cosmic mind, pure and unlimited, now flows through me, giving me awareness of the pattern of my future destiny.

After this woman had meditated on the problems that afflicted her life, she began to get a glimmer of soul perception, and with her new regime of Mind Cosmology, she went on to become a changed person. She became healed of her various ailments, and now is awaiting the unfoldment of her destiny with serenity and confidence.

6. Now you are ready for the soul's second stage of unfolding in the light of truth. This is the meditation on the soul's investigation of reality.

As you sit silently in meditation ask your higher mind: What is reality? How can you be guided and helped by the soul's awareness? Is your body real, or does spirit govern and control the physical self? Can you overcome pain and worry and anxiety about the future?

As you sit quietly in the silence holding each of these questions in the forefront of consciousness, your soul, which knows the mysteries behind life, will project to your higher psychic centers the true answers to your questions.

7. Also, ask this higher soul how to solve your problems. Where you should live, what work you should do, whom you should marry, where to earn the money you need. The soul has awareness not only of spiritual matters, but of how you should live your life in every way. As you sit silently, concentrating your mind on this higher spiritual center, you will be guided by intuition and psychic guidance to the working out of your problems. The soul has the divine qualities of omniscience, omnipotence and omnipresence. It knows all, is all-powerful and is everywhere present, as infinite intelligence, at all times, and is available to you and your questing mind for giving you aid to the baffling problems of life.

A woman in our lecture work needed a sum of money by a certain date, and she turned in desperation to the higher spiritual mind that she had learned could help her. Within two days a letter came with a check for the exact amount she needed!

A man, who had studied these laws of Mind Cosmology, lost his wallet, in which he had an airplane ticket, three hundred dollars in cash and all his identification papers. He knew that the person finding it could easily keep the cash and never return it. But he went into soul reverie and asked his higher spiritual mind to contact the person finding his valuables and impress upon him the urgency of returning it.

The very next day the telephone rang, and a man told him he had found his wallet and would return it that same day! He gave the finder a generous reward, and believes firmly that something in his soul reached out and touched the finder's soul with the message to return his valuables.

8. Man's soul may communicate with the soul of the universe, which we call God's creative mind in action, through the powerful medium of prayer and faith.

Whenever you want soul inspiration and light, go to the cosmic source of all life, light, intelligence, good and power. In your prayers ask for divine guidance. Give thanks for the past blessings that God has given you. Have faith that this Father within can hear your requests and will grant them.

9. The soul responds to man's highest aspirations and inspiration. Go into meditation daily and achieve a state of inner rapture and ecstasy, in which you elevate your consciousness through mystic contemplation of the divine soul and its purpose in this mystical journey of life.

You can achieve this form of high spiritual inspiration by contemplating beauty in nature; by viewing magnificent classical paintings from the masters; by being aware of sunrises and sunsets, in which the heavens are aflame with the glory of God. See the mystery and beauty of the universe all around you and then let that beauty and inspiration enter into your consciousness and become a part of your higher inspiration.

Another way by which your soul reaches that state of rapture, which is called nirvana, is to sit quietly in meditation with beautiful classical music playing, and candlelight. As you meditate on the sacred flame, and listen to the inspirational music from a Beethoven, Mozart, Chopin, Handel or some other composer whose music has lasted for a century or more, let your spirits soar, and feel that your soul is rising into the transcendental realms of pure, infinite spirit. At such times you will have a soaring sensation, as though rising above the earth plane into the pure spiritual stratosphere of God's infinite peace, infinite good, infinite beauty, infinite intelligence, and infinite love.

It is in such moments of divine inspiration that your soul will feel itself coalescing with the soul of the universe, and you will be aware of the music of the spheres, and the transcendental joy that comes to those who are illumined. You will then have achieved the fulfillment for which your soul has searched since the beginning of time. Your life will then take on new purpose and meaning and you will never again be limited by the mortal mind consciousness that keeps people earthbound. You will be on your way to the stars, sustained by this golden philosophy of mystic revelation.

Use these truths of Mind Cosmology wisely and well. You will reap immeasurable benefits from these transcendental truths that will make your life magnificent and triumphant!

SUMMARY OF CHAPTER TWENTY

1. The mystical purpose behind your life and the soul's triumphal journey through time and space, for achieving mastery over life and circumstances.

2. The mystical properties of your soul and how you may tap this tremendous spiritual power in the fourth dimensional realm.

3. How you may use the soul's mystic properties to achieve cosmic fulfillment, Darshan, the ancient Sanskrit word meaning ultimate fulfillment.

4. How Mr. T. L. violated cosmic laws and suffered a physical breakdown, and how he was healed with a regime of Mind Cosmology and spiritual therapy.

5. The first stage of soul enlightenment and how you can overcome fear, worry, problems of health, and premature aging and death through the soul's guidance.

6. How one woman who lived in discord, friction and negativity was able to overcome her problems and start on the pathway of a new life through this study of soul evolvement.

7. The second stage of the soul's mystical unfoldment, through meditation on what is reality, and how to overcome life's burdens and problems.

8. How the soul can actually help overcome problems of health, business and finances, and how one woman received a sum of money by a certain time when she sought spiritual help.

9. How a man used these laws to reach out and touch the soul of a man who had found his wallet with three hundred dollars cash, an airplane ticket and all his papers.

10. How to use the power of prayer and faith to contact the soul of the universe and use it to achieve anything in life that you desire.

11. How to use the soul's divine inspiration to be aware of the tremendous forces that are alive within the universe, and be inspired by the beauty in nature, by beautiful music and high levels of inspiring poetry, literature, and art.